AMERICAN FOREIGN POLICY

OPPOSING VIEWPOINTS

GARY E. McCUEN
DAVID L. BENDER
(Editors)

GREENHAVEN PRESS - ANOKA, MINNESOTA 55303

© COPYRIGHT 1972 by GREENHAVEN PRESS
ISBN 0-912616-05-9 PAPER EDITION
ISBN 0-912616-30-X CLOTH EDITION

Table of Contents

Table of Exercises

SELF-INTEREST AND IDEALISM

Readings:
1. Morality and International Politics
   Arthur Schlesinger, Jr.
2. U.S. Policy Should be Guided by Idealism
   Robert Endicott Osgood

MORALITY AND
INTERNATIONAL POLITICS

by Arthur Schlesinger, Jr.*

(Mr. Schlesinger is currently Albert Schweitzer Professor of Humanities at The City University of New York. He has won many literary and academic awards over the years, including a Pulitzer Prize for History in 1945. He was a special assistant to President Kennedy from 1961-1964 and is the author of many books, most of them dealing with history and politics.)

Consider the following questions while reading:

1. How does Schlesinger feel moral principles should be involved in our decision to fight in Vietnam?
2. Why does Schlesinger feel that nations are not bound by the same moral principles that bind individuals? Do you agree?
3. What danger of fanaticism does Schlesinger see in nations whose foreign policy decisions are made on a moral basis?

*Arthur Schlesinger, Jr., "The Necessary Amorality of Foreign Affairs," *Harpers,* August, 1971, pp. 72-74. Copyright © 1971, by Minneapolis Star and Tribune Co., Inc. Reprinted from the August, 1971 issue of Harper's Magazine by permission of the author.

For centuries, theologians have distinguished between just and unjust wars, jurists have propounded rules for international conduct, and moralists have worried whether their own nation's course in foreign affairs was right or wrong. Yet the problem of the relationship between morality and international politics remains perennially unsettled. It is particularly difficult and disturbing for Americans today. The Indochina war was first widely justified on moral grounds and is now widely condemned on moral grounds. Both judgments cannot be right. This contradiction and, even more, of course, the shame and horror of the war must surely compel us to look again at the moral question in its relation to foreign policy. ...

Should — as both supporters and critics of the Indochina war have asserted — overt moral principles decide issues of foreign policy? Required to give a succinct answer, I am obliged to say: as little as possible. If, in the management of foreign affairs, decisions can be made and questions disposed of on other grounds, so much the better. Moral values in international politics — or so, at least, my temperament enjoins me to believe — should be decisive only in questions of last resort. One must add that questions of last resort do exist. ...

The argument for the application of moral principles to questions of foreign policy is thus that there is, or should be, an identity between the morality of individuals and the morality of states. The issues involved here are not easy. Clearly, there are cases in foreign affairs where moral judgment is possible and necessary. But I suggest that these are extreme cases and do not warrant the routine use of moral criteria in making foreign-policy decisions. It was to expose such indiscriminate moralism that Reinhold Niebuhr wrote *Moral Man and Immoral Society* forty years ago. The passage of time has not weakened the force of his analysis.

Niebuhr insisted on the distinction between the moral behavior of individuals and of social groups. The obligation of the individual was to obey the law of love and sacrifice; "from the viewpoint of the author of an action, unselfishness must remain the criterion of the highest morality." But nations cannot be sacrificial. Governments are not individuals. They are trustees for individuals. Niebuhr quotes Hugh Cecil's argument that unselfishness "is inappropriate to the action of a state. No one has a right to be unselfish with other people's interests." Alexander Hamilton made the same point in the early years

3

of the American republic: "The rule of morality ... is not precisely the same between nations as between individuals. The duty of making its own welfare the guide of its actions is much stronger upon the former than upon the latter. Existing millions, and for the most part future generations, are concerned in the present measures of a government; while the consequences of the private action of an individual ordinarily terminate with himself, or are circumscribed with a narrow compass."

In short, the individual's duty of self-sacrifice and the nation's duty of self-preservation are in conflict; and this makes it impossible to measure the action of nations by a purely individualistic morality. "The Sermon on the Mount," said Churchill, "is the last word in Christian ethics. ... Still, it is not on those terms that Ministers assume their responsibilities of guiding states." Saints can be pure, but statesmen must be responsible. As trustees for others, they must defend interests and compromise principles. In politics, practical and prudential judgment must have priority over moral verdicts. ...

A nation's law can set down relatively clear standards of right and wrong in individual behavior because it is the product of an imperfect but nonetheless authentic internal moral consensus. International life has no such broad or deep moral consensus. It was once hoped that modern technology would create a common fund of moral ideas transcending the interests of particular nations — common concepts of interest, justice, and comity — either because the revolution in communications would bring people together through hope of mutual understanding or because the revolution in weapons would bring them together through fear of mutual destruction. Such expectations have been disappointed. Until nations come to adopt the same international morality, there can be no world law to regulate the behavior of states. Nor can international institutions — the League of Nations or the United Nations — produce by sleight of hand a moral consensus where none exists. World law must express world community; it cannot create it. ...

It is not only that moral principles are of limited use in the conduct of foreign affairs. It is also that the compulsion to see foreign policy in moral terms may have, with the noblest of intentions, the most ghastly of consequences. The moralization of foreign affairs encourages, for example, a misunderstanding of the nature of foreign policy. Moralists tend to prefer symbolic to substantive politics.

4

They tend to see foreign policy as a means not of influencing events but of registering virtuous attitudes. One has only to recall the attempt, made variously by Right and by Left, to make recognition policy an instrument of ethical approval or disapproval.

Step Carefully

A deeper trouble is inherent in the very process of pronouncing moral judgment of foreign policy. For the man who converts conflicts of interest and circumstance into conflicts of good and evil necessarily invests himself with moral superiority. Those who see foreign affairs as made up of questions of right and wrong begin by supposing they know better than other people what is right for them. The more passionately they believe they are right, the more likely they are to reject expediency and accommodation and seek the final victory of their principles. Little has been more pernicious in international politics than excessive righteousness. ...

Moralism in foreign policy ends up in fanaticism, and the fanatic, as Mr. Dooley put it, "does what he thinks th' Lord wud do if He only knew th' facts in th' case." Abroad it leads to crusades and the extermination of the infidel; at home it perceives mistakes in political judgment as evidence of moral obliquity. The issue becomes not self-delusion or stupidity but criminality and treachery; ferreting out the reprobate as traitors or war criminals becomes the goal. Those who are convinced of their own superior righteousness should recall Chekhov's warning: "You will not become a saint through other people's sins."

If moral principles have only limited application to foreign policy, then we are forced to the conclusion that decisions in foreign affairs must generally be taken on other than moralistic grounds. What are these other grounds? ...

The safest basis for foreign policy lies not in attempts to determine what is right or wrong but in attempts to determine the national interest. ...

A moment's thought will show that every nation *must* respond to some sense of its national interest, for a nation that rejects national interest as the mainspring of its policy cannot survive. Without the magnetic compass of national interest, there would be no regularity and predictability in international affairs. George Washington called it "a maxim founded on the universal experience of mankind that no nation is to be trusted farther than it is bound by its interest." ...

National interest has a self-limiting factor. It cannot, unless transformed by an injection of moral righteousness, produce ideological crusades for unlimited objectives. Any consistent defender of the idea of national interest must concede that other nations have legitimate interests too, and this sets bounds on international conflict. "You can compromise interests," Hans Morgenthau has reminded us, "but you cannot compromise principles." ...

Uncontrolled national egoism generally turns out to be contrary to long-term national interest. Can it be

6

Is this the real Uncle Sam?

persuasively held, for example, that Hitler's foreign policy was in the national interest of Germany? The imperialist states of nineteenth-century Europe have generally been forced to revise their notions as to where national interest truly lies. In time this may even happen to the Soviet Union and the United States.

National interest, realistically construed, will promote enlightened rather than greedy policy. So a realist like Hamilton said (my emphasis) that his aim was not "to recommend a policy absolutely selfish or interested in nations; but to show, that a policy regulated by their own interest, *as far as justice and good faith permit,* is, and ought to be, their prevailing one." And a realist like Theodore Roosevelt could say: "It is neither wise nor right for a nation to disregard its own needs, and it is foolish — and may be wicked — to think that other nations will disregard theirs. But it is wicked for a nation only to regard its own interest, and foolish to believe that such is the sole motive that actuates any other nation. It should be our steady aim to raise the ethical standard of national action just as we strive to raise the ethical standard of individual action."

7

U.S. POLICY SHOULD
BE GUIDED BY IDEALISM

by Robert Endicott Osgood*

(Robert Endicott Osgood is an educator and the author of several books in the field of foreign affairs. He is an expert on foreign affairs and has lectured and taught in this field in the United States and in Europe.)

Use the following questions to assist you in your reading:

1. Why does the author of this reading feel that it would harm our country internally to ignore moral principles in making foreign policy decisions?
2. Mr. Osgood claims that we Americans are unable to make foreign policy decisions solely on a basis of self-interest. What is his reasoning?
3. Why does the author feel that idealism is as much an instrument of national power as the weapons of war?

*Robert Endicott Osgood, *Ideals and Self-Interest in America's Foreign Relations* (Chicago: University of Chicago Press, 1953), pp. 443-51. Copyright 1953 by the University of Chicago.

> "It is a very perilous thing to determine the foreign policy of a nation in the terms of material interest. It not only is unfair to those with whom you are dealing, but it is degrading as regards your own actions. ...
>
> We dare not turn from the principle that morality and not expediency is the thing that must guide us and that we will never condone iniquity because it is most convenient to do so."

President Woodrow Wilson at Mobile, Alabama, October 27, 1913

SELF-INTEREST WITHOUT IDEALS IS SELF-DEFEATING

If one assumes the worth of the Christian-liberal-humanitarian ideals, as this essay does, then it is relevant to understand that the calculation and pursuit of national self-interest without regard for universal ideals is not only immoral but self-defeating. ...

If American power becomes an end in itself, American society, no less than international society, will suffer; for unless American security is measured by ideal standards transcending the national interest, it may take forms that undermine the moral basis of all social relations. If the Christian, humanitarian, and democratic values, which are the basis of America's social and political institutions, are valid at all, they are as valid outside American borders as within. Consequently, if they cease to compel respect in America's foreign relations, they will, ultimately, become ineffective in her domestic affairs. The resulting destruction of America's moral fiber through the loss of national integrity and the disintegration of ethical standards would be as great a blow to the nation as an armed attack upon her territory. ...

HUMAN NATURE DEMANDS THAT IDEALS SUPPLEMENT REASON

A view of international relations which imagines that nations can in the long run achieve a stable and effective foreign policy solely by a rational calculation of the demands of national self-interest is based upon an unrealistic conception of human nature, for it is certainly utopian to expect any great number of people to have the wit to perceive or the will to follow the dictates of enlightened self-interest on the basis of sheer reason alone. Rational self-interest divorced from ideal principles is as weak and erratic a guide for foreign policy as idealism undisciplined by reason. No great mass of people is Machiavellian, least of all the American people. Americans in particular have displayed a strong aversion to the pursuit of self-interest, unless self-interest has been leavened with moral sentiment.

A genuine realist should recognize that the transcendent ideals expressed in the traditional American mission, no less than America's fundamental strategic interest, are an indispensable source of stability in America's foreign relations. ...

THE EXPEDIENCY OF IDEALISM

A true realist must recognize that ideals and self-interest are so closely interdependent that, even on grounds of national expediency, there are cogent arguments for maintaining the vitality of American idealism.

Ideals are as much an instrument of national power as the weapons of war. All manifestations of national power, including the threat of coercion, operate by influencing the thoughts and actions of human beings, whether by frightening them or by converting them. Since men are motivated by faith and moral sentiment as well as by fear and the instinct of self-preservation, the strength of America's moral reputation and the persuasiveness of the American mission are as vital a factor in the power equation as planes, ships, and tanks. One has only to recall the consequences of the rise and fall of America's moral reputation during and after World War I to understand the force of American idealism among foreign peoples.

The persuasiveness of the American mission is especially significant under the present circumstances, when the competition of ideologies is such a conspicuous feature of the power struggle between the Russian and the American orbits and when the effectiveness of American policy depends so heavily upon winning the moral and intellectual allegiance of vast numbers of people in the throes of social and nationalistic revolution. If in the eyes of millions of people living in underdeveloped areas of the

"Oh wad some power the giftie gie us to see oursels as others see us"
—Robert Burns

world the United States ceases to stand for a positive and constructive program of social and material progress, if American ideals no longer mean anything beyond smug generalities and hypocritical rationalizations of selfish national advantage, then all the wealth and military power the United States can muster will not render these people an asset to the free world. If the nations within the Western Coalition conclude that America has lost all passion for improving the lot of common people for the sake of the people themselves, if they believe that Americans have lost interest in the vision of world peace in their over-riding concern for their national self-interest, then no display of shrewd power politics will win for the United States the popular trust and admiration which American leadership requires.

THE MORAL RESPONSIBILITY OF NATIONAL LEADERS*

The same natural law, which governs relations between individual human beings, must also regulate the relations of political communities with one another.

This will be readily understood when one reflects that the individual representatives of political communities cannot put aside their personal dignity while they are acting in the name and interest of their countries; and that they cannot therefore violate the very law of nature by which they are bound, which is itself the moral law.

It would be absurd, moreover, even to imagine that men could surrender their own human attributes, or be compelled to do so, by the very fact of their appointment to public office. Rather, they have been given that noble assignment precisely because the wealth of their human endowments has earned them their reputation as outstanding members of the body politic.

Furthermore, authority to govern is a necessary requirement of the moral order in civil society. It may not be used against that order; and the very instant such an attempt were made, it would cease to bind. For the Lord Himself has warned: *Hear, therefore, kings, and understand; learn, you magistrates of the earth's expanse! Hearken, you who rule the multitude and lord it over throngs of peoples! Because authority was given you by the Lord and sovereignty by the Most High, who shall probe your works and scrutinize your counsels!* (Wisdom 6, 2-4).

---

*Pope John XXIII, PACEM IN TERRIS, ed. William J. Gibbons, S.J. (Glen Rock, N.J.: Paulist Press, 1963), pp. 31-32. Reprinted with permission from Paulist/Newman Press.

Moreover, no coalition can survive through a common fear of tyranny without a common faith in liberty. If the leader of the Western Coalition ceases to sustain that faith, then who will sustain it? Because the United States is unavoidably thrust into a position of global leadership, her standards of conduct must, inevitably, have a great influence in setting the moral tone of international relations in general. Consequently, it behooves America to conduct its foreign relations in a way that will encourage the kind of international environment compatible with its ideals and interests.

ABILITY TO EMPATHIZE

The ability to empathize, to see a problem from another person's vantage point, is a skill that must be widely developed and practiced in order for the world to solve disputes peacefully. Read the following statements that present different views about morality and aggression in world politics. Then decide which statement you think is the most difficult to empathize with.

A. "I take it for granted that every intelligent person realizes that America could not long survive as a free nation in a world completely or near-completely Communist. I take it for granted that every patriotic American, no matter what position he has taken on Vietnam, would agree on the essential point that, somehow, we must draw the line against further communist expansion — in Asia, in Africa, in the Mideast, and in Latin America."[1]

B. "Our policy, Pusey declares, is 'Globalism running riot' and a denial of traditional American goals. We oppose communism because it tries 'to impose its will on people by force and terror.' Yet, 'we ourselves construct the greatest complex of military bastions in all history. ...' Sen. Symington observed, 'We are the self-appointed babysitters of the world, and could be going broke doing it."[2]

C. "To most of the world's people, the white man it seems is the bad one. He is the man who moved in on their ancestors, slaughtered many of them, captured them, sold them into slavery, exploited their natural resources for his own benefit ... and this is overwhelmingly the common feeling about the white man practically all over the world."[3]

---

[1] Senator Thomas J. Dodd, *Congressional Record,* February 26, 1968.

[2] Boyd C. Shafer, "Babysitter of the Globe ... America," *Minneapolis Tribune,* September 12, 1971, p. 9D. This article is a review of Merlo J. Pusey's book, *The U.S.A. Astride The Globe.*

[3] Dr. Brock Chisholm (former Director General, the World Health Organization), Senate Foreign Relations Committee, May 5, 1969.

1. Which statement is the easiest for you to empathize with? The most difficult?

2. Now try to imagine which of the above statements each of the following individuals would most easily identify with:
   a. Senator George McGovern
   b. Governor George Wallace
   c. President Lyndon Johnson
   d. President Richard Nixon
   e. Eldridge Cleaver
   f. Premier Fidel Castro of Cuba
   g. Chairman Mao Tse Tung of Communist China
   h. Vice President Spiro Agnew
   i. Senator Hubert Humphrey
   j. Ralph Nader
   k. President Anwar Sadat of Egypt
   l. Premier Eisaka Sato of Japan
   m. Premier Alexei Kosygin of Russia
   n. Premier Golda Meir of Israel

3. Now examine the following cartoon. Which of the above individuals would be most likely to agree with the cartoon's message? Why?

SECOND THOUGHTS!

MINNEAPOLIS STAR

15

THE GOALS OF AMERICAN FOREIGN POLICY

READING NUMBER 3

U.S. GOAL
IS WORLDWIDE FREEDOM

by Dean Rusk*

(Dean Rusk was Secretary of the Department of State from 1961 - 1969 under presidents Kennedy and Johnson. He previously held other government positions in the field of international relations. He has also taught political science and served as the president of the Rockefeller Foundation.)

As you read try to answer the following questions:

1. What does Secretary Rusk mean when he speaks of worldwide freedom?
2. What does Secretary Rusk see as the primary purpose of our military power?
3. How are our foreign policy objectives in South Vietnam described?
4. How do Communist China and Russia relate to U.S. foreign policy objectives in Secretary Rusk's analysis?

*Address by the Secretary of State before The Veterans of Foreign Wars Convention, New York, August 22, 1966. Taken from *American Foreign Policy: Current Documents, 1966,* by the U.S. Department of State, pp. 21-25.

Four years ago ... I discussed the goal of American foreign policy.[1] I called our goal "a worldwide victory for freedom." And I described it this way:

"A world free of aggression — aggression by whatever means.

"A world of independent nations, each with the institutions of its own choice but cooperating with one another to their mutual advantage.

"A world which yields continuing progress in economic and social justice for all peoples.

"A world which provides sure and equitable means for the peaceful settlement of disputes and moves progressively toward a rule of law which lays down and enforces standards of conduct in relations between nations.

"A world in which, in the great tradition shared by peoples in every continent, governments derive 'their just powers from the consent of the governed.'

"A world in which the powers of the state over the individual are limited by law, practice, and custom — in which the personal freedoms essential to the dignity of man are secure."

As I said 4 years ago, we must try to achieve that goal without a great war, although, as I said also, "... we will defend our vital interests and those of the free world by whatever means may be necessary. ..."

Our goal remains unchanged. And that is as it should be. For our goal springs from the basic commitments we made to ourselves and to history at our birth as a nation. It expresses aspirations that are shared by men and women in every part of the earth. It cannot be allowed to remain just a dream. For it represents the most vital interests of mankind — the kind of world order which must be achieved if civilization, or even the human race, is to survive in the age of intercontinental rockets with thermonuclear warheads. ...

The first essential in organizing a peaceful world is to eliminate aggression. The primary purpose of our military forces is to make resort to force by the adversaries of freedom unprofitable and dangerous. Our nuclear deterrent

[1]Text in *American Foreign Policy: Current Documents, 1962*, pp. 30-37.

"Our foreign policy must always be an extension of this nation's domestic policy. Our safest guide to what we do abroad is always to take a good look at what we are doing at home."

President Lyndon Johnson at the University of Denver, August 26, 1966.

has been vastly strengthened. The destructive capacity of the super-weapons is almost unimaginable. I believe that all governments in the world must surely recognize that to initiate a thermonuclear exchange would be a wholly irrational act.

I believe also that it is recognized very widely, if not universally, that aggression by masses of conventional forces moving across frontiers is far too reckless an act for the world in which we now live.

But there is a third type of aggression — what the Communists, in their inverted jargon, call "wars of national liberation." As I said at your convention in Minneapolis 4 years ago: "This is the form of the present aggression against South Viet-Nam. And it will not be allowed to succeed." ...

Our objective in South Viet-Nam and Southeast Asia, as in the rest of the world, is peace — a peace which permits independent peoples to live in freedom under governments and institutions of their own choice. We have sought with the utmost persistence to bring the other side to the conference table. We shall continue to explore every possibility of an honorable peace. But we will not be driven out of South Viet-Nam by aggressive force. And we will not agree to a settlement that does not assure to the people of South Viet-Nam their right to peace and a free choice.

The Government of the United States, under four successive Presidents, reached the considered judgment that the defense of Southeast Asia is very important to the security of the free world, including the United States.

19

Nearly 12 years ago, this judgment was reinforced when we solemnly committed ourselves by treaty to the defense of certain countries of Southeast Asia, including South Viet-Nam. Our defensive alliances are the backbone of world peace. It is imperative that our adversaries and our friends know that the United States will do what it promises to do.

Because the other side has escalated the aggression against South Viet-Nam, we and others have been compelled to increase our assistance. We will do our share of whatever may be necessary to prevent the seizure of South Viet-Nam by force. ...

Our firm support of South Viet-Nam has already yielded important dividends. Throughout the western Pacific, governments and peoples now know that the advance of communism in Asia has been challenged and that the United States has the will and the means to make good on its pledges. As a result, the free nations of the area are moving forward with new confidence. ...

The Republic of Korea is forging ahead. And it continues to make large contributions to the defense of security and peace in Asia. The Republic of China on Taiwan continues its remarkable economic and social advance. It is now rendering technical assistance to more than 25 countries. Thailand and Malaysia and the Philippines are making impressive gains. ...

Australia and New Zealand are showing exciting progress; we are glad to have them as stanch allies as we face with them common threats.

Indonesia has decisively defeated an attempted Communist takeover and taken the first steps toward reviving its potentially rich economy. It has signed an agreement with Malaysia laying the basis for cooperation to replace conflict between these two countries. Under sound leadership Indonesia can become a prosperous nation and a nonaligned bastion of freedom in Asia.

The free nations of Asia and the western Pacific are coming together in various promising cooperative undertakings. The new Asian Development Bank, with 31 members, which will hold its first meeting in October, will further stimulate economic growth in Asia. Japan took the lead in convening a conference on Southeast Asian development. Development of the lower Mekong Valley is proceeding despite the war. Korea took the lead in bringing together representatives of 10 nations, at which ASPAC (the Asian and Pacific Council) was founded. The Philippines, Malaysia, and Thailand are strengthening the Association for Southeast Asia.

An important element in the progress of the free nations of Asia has been the declining position and influence of Communist China. Its attacks on Tibet and India, its support of the aggression against South Viet-Nam, and its militant doctrine have destroyed its claim to be a peace-loving state. The collapse of the "great leap forward" punctured its claims to be a model for developing states seeking rapid economic growth. Today, the growing gap in living standards between the China mainland and neighboring Asian states is convincing evidence that free societies have more to offer their citizens. ...

Eventually mainland China may have leaders who realize that aggression is a losing game and that they have more to gain from joining in cooperative endeavors with their neighbors of Asia and the Pacific. As President Johnson emphasized in his speech of July 12, a peaceful China is essential to lasting peace in Asia, and the United States is seeking ways to breach the wall of hostility which now separates the American people from our historic friends, the people of mainland China.

On the other side of the world the nations of the Atlantic constitute, as they have for so many years, the center of world industrial and military power. Power of such magnitude has a vast potential for good or evil. Where great powers live closely together there is always danger of conflict, and it is no accident that the two great wars of modern times have begun in Europe. Today, 20 years after the war, Europe remains divided, and it is an urgent piece of unfinished business to end the division of Europe and, in particular, to secure the reunification of Germany.

These tasks must remain high-priority items on the agenda of free nations. Until they can be accomplished, world stability will not be finally secured.

Yet to bring about an end to this dangerous division, the Western nations must remain strong and cohesive. During the last 20 years great strides have been made to achieve this. Six of the Western European nations have gone very far toward the integration of their economies. This has enabled them to take advantage of the benefits of a mass market, and, as a result, their peoples are today enjoying a standard of living they have never known before.

21

Our own attitude is — and will continue to be — to encourage the development of unity in Europe to encompass not only the present members of the European Communities but Great Britain and other nations as well. ...

The United States stands ready to act as a friendly partner of a uniting Europe just as, during the last decade and a half, we have worked with Europeans on the hard tasks of a common defense. Together we have built a great alliance. To give it reality, we have constructed an effective collective defense system. ...

The objectives of cohesion among the Atlantic nations are not limited to defense or even to deterrence. Through common action we must create those conditions in which, over time, a European settlement can be achieved. Such a settlement to be lasting must be based on principles of equality. It must be willingly accepted. It must give to all peoples concerned the assurance that their vital interests are protected.

A lasting settlement will require changes in the attitude of the Soviet Government. Such changes as have already occurred have not come through the independent action of individual Western states. They have occurred in part because of internal shifts and movements within the Soviet system. But equally as important, they have occurred because the Western Powers have created conditions to which the Soviet Union has found it necessary to adjust.

We must continue, therefore, to work for the conditions that will make it possible for Europe to be reunited, with neither the Atlantic powers nor the nations of the Warsaw Pact seeing in that happy event any threat to themselves. For this reason the United States has committed itself to a policy of peaceful exploration of better relations with the countries of Eastern Europe and the Soviet Union. Ours is not an effort to subvert the Eastern European governments nor to make those states hostile to the Soviet Union or to each other. No one would benefit from an Eastern Europe that is again balkanized. We wish to build bridges to the East so that the Soviet Union and the Eastern European states can begin to see a genuine interest for themselves in moving toward better relations with the West and toward ending the partition of Europe and Germany.

This is a good policy for everyone. For all of us — Americans, Russians, Europeans — can benefit from drawing closer together. In that way we can reduce the risks of war, minimize the bitter legacies of national conflict, and increase the tangible fruits of economic cooperation. In that way we can make it possible for the wealth and talent which Europe, the United States, and the Soviet Union have in such abundance to serve the cause of humanity. What we thus desire for Europe, we firmly believe, is what Europeans want. And that is why America and Europe remain so relevant to each other's future.

In the Western Hemisphere ... we have been working closely with our Latin American partners at accelerating economic and social development and strengthening democratic institutions. ...

For every dollar that the United States has contributed, our Alliance partners have invested almost five in their programs for economic and social progress. The Alliance, then, is a true partnership, with self-help by our Latin American friends playing the primary role. Most important, the Alliance offers the prospect of peaceful change through constructive, democratic processes as an alternative to change through the destructive extremism offered by the Communists. With the Alliance, the people of this hemisphere have rejected the Castro alternative, and communism has lost much of its appeal. Castro's Cuba is mired in an economic morass, despite large-scale aid from the Soviet Union.

With few exceptions the nations of the region now have freely elected governments. We cooperated with the OAS (Organization of American States) in preventing chaos and a possible Communist takeover in the Dominican Republic, and that country now enjoys a government freely chosen by its own people.

THE HYPOCRISY
OF AMERICAN FOREIGN POLICY

by Henry Steele Commager*

(Henry Steele Commager is an educator and lecturer, and is currently a professor of history at Amherst College. He has earned many honors for his work in the United States and in other nations. He is also the author of many books in the field of history, including *The Growth of the American Republic, The American Mind* and *The Heritage of America.*)

As you read consider the following questions:

1. What criticism does Mr. Commager have of America's westward expansion during our early history?
2. The author suggests that communism has corrupted American society. What is his point?
3. Mr. Commager accuses us of practicing a double standard of morality in our dealings with other nations. Do you agree with him?

*Henry Steele Commager, "A Historian Looks at Our Political Morality," *Saturday Review*, July 10, 1965, pp. 16-18. Copyright 1965 Saturday Review, Inc. Reprinted with the permission of Saturday Review, Inc. and the author.

"Every philosophy," wrote Alfred North Whitehead, "is tinged with the coloring of some secret, imaginative background, which never emerges explicitly in its train of reasoning." True enough — though *never* is a pretty strong word here. What is the secret, or perhaps the inarticulate imaginative background, that colors American thinking about relations with other peoples and nations in the past and today? Is it not the once explicit and openly avowed, but now implicit assumption of American superiority, both material and moral, especially to lesser breeds without our law? Is it not the assumption that America is somehow outside the workings of history, exempt from such laws as may govern history?

The origin of this attitude traces back to the generation that created the new nation and came to think of that nation as a people apart. It is rooted in the long-popular notion of New World innocence and Old World corruption, New World virtue and Old World vice, a notion that runs like a red thread through the whole of our literature from Benjamin Franklin to Henry James, and through our politics and diplomacy as well. It is connected with the convulsive fact of physical removal — the uprooting and transplanting to new and more fertile soil, with the phenomenon of a continuous westward emigration from the Old World, while so few went eastward across the ocean. It is related to the American priority in independence and in nation-making, with the glowing achievements of the new nation — religious freedom, for example, the end to colonialism, the classless society — and over the years it was strengthened by the argument of special destiny, and by the experience of abundance and freedom from Old World wars, and of growth even beyond the dreams of the Founding Fathers. No wonder the notion of a special providence and a special destiny caught the American imagination.

Something was to be said for all this in the early years of the Republic, when the American world was not only new but brave. Rather less was to be said for it as the nineteenth century wore on — the century that saw the new nation indulge in so many of the follies of the older nations: slavery, racial and religious intolerance, the disparity between rich and poor, civil war, imperialism, and foreign wars.

But even in the nineteenth century, perhaps especially in the nineteenth century, Americans developed the habit of brushing aside whatever was embarrassing that still characterizes them, the habit of taking for granted a double standard of history and morality. There were, to be sure, awkward things in our history, but somehow they were not to be held against us, somehow they didn't count. The conquest and decimation of the Indian didn't count — after all, the Indians were heathens — and when that argument lost its force, there was the undeniable charge that they got in the way of progress. The students of my own college celebrate Lord Jeffrey Amherst on all ceremonial occasions, but few of them remember that Lord Amherst's solution to the Indian problem was to send the Indians blankets infected with smallpox! How many of us, after all, remember what Helen Hunt Jackson called a "Century of Dishonor"? Or there was slavery; it was pervasive and flourishing, and slaveholders defended it as a moral good. Somehow slavery didn't count, either, because it was nature's way of bringing the African to Western civilization, or because it was all so romantic (only recently have we developed a sense of guilt here).

AMERICA, A THREAT TO WORLD PEACE

To most Europeans, I guess, America now looks like the most dangerous country in the world. Since America is unquestionably the most powerful country, the transformation of America's image within the last 30 years is very frightening for Europeans.

It is probably still more frightening for the great majority of the human race who are neither Europeans nor North Americans, but are Latin Americans, Asians and Africans.

THEY, I imagine, feel even more insecure than we feel. They feel that, at any moment, America may intervene in their internal affairs with the same appalling consequences as have followed from American intervention in Southeast Asia.

Arnold J. Toynbee, a British historian.

The Industrial Revolution, too, brought in its train most of the evils that afflicted Europe in these same stormy years, but that could all be put down as the price of progress, which is just what Herbert Spencer and his infatuated American followers did. And surely no one could assert that the price was too high. So, too, with what, in other nations, would be called imperialism, but with us was called "westward expansion" — manifest destiny working itself out in some foreordained fashion. The Mexicans do not take quite this view of the matter, but that has not troubled us. Even now we do not inquire quite as closely into the war-guilt question for the Mexican War, or the war with Spain, or the Filipino war, as we do for the Franco-Prussian War or World War I. ...

We are no longer quite so sure of the New World innocence and Old World corruption as in the past — sometimes we suspect it may be the other way around — but the older notions of American superiority, and of the exemption of America from the familiar processes of history persist. They were very much in the mind of Woodrow Wilson when he prepared to make the world safe for democracy. But then the world we made did not suit us at all; clearly we had been betrayed by the wicked diplomats of the Old World. We cut our losses and withdrew into isolation and watched the Old World destroy itself with a kind of malign satisfaction, meanwhile congratulating ourselves that we were not involved and that our irresponsibility was really a form of moral superiority.

For we were very sure of our own virtue, and we read history to discover that we were a peculiar people. Our history books exalted everything American. They contrasted our Indian policy with the wicked policy of the Spaniards — that was part of the black legend — conveniently overlooking the elementary fact that the Indian survived in Mexico and South America but not in the United States. They painted slavery as a romantic institution, or perhaps as a kind of fortunate accident for the Africans. They even ascribed the exceeding bounty of nature not to providence or to luck but to our own virtue. In recent years many of our spokesmen commit the vulgar error of identifying an economy based on unrestricted exploitation of natural abundance as "the American way of life," and of scorning less fortunate people for having fewer resources and a different, and obviously inferior, way of life. We forget Reinhold Niebuhr's admonishment that "The more we indulge in uncritical reverence for the supposed wisdom of the American way of life, the more odious we make it in the eyes of the world, and the more we destroy our moral authority. ..."

During the great war we responded, generously and

27

unselfishly, to the challenge that confronted us; this was, in a sense, our finest hour, too: Lend-Lease, the alliance with Britain, the acceptance of the Soviet as an ally in the struggle against tyranny, the Atlantic Charter and the United Nations and the far-sighted Marshall Plan, the response to the challenge of aggression in Korea. But the rising threat of Communism did what the actual attack by Nazi and Fascist powers had been unable to do. The prolonged struggle with Communism, which we sometimes call the Cold War, accentuated our innate sense of superiority. To vast numbers of Americans it justified — and apparently still does justify — resort to almost any weapons or conduct. For years now we have heard, and not from extremists alone, that the struggle between democracy and Communism is the struggle between Light and Darkness, Good and Evil, and that the moral distinction is an absolute one.

The arguments that were invoked to justify religious wars and religious persecution in past centuries are invoked now to justify sleepless hostility to Communism — even preventive war. Happily, the extremists have not had their way in the conduct of foreign policy, but we know how effective they have been on the domestic scene, how they have denounced as traitors those who do not agree with them and persecuted them with relentless venom, how they have poisoned public life, and private, too, preaching hatred of Russia, hatred of Cuba, hatred of China — hatred directed toward all those who do not agree with them and with their easy remedies. Those hate-mongers, sure of themselves and of their moral superiority, have not hesitated to ignore law and the Constitution when it suited their book or to lie and cheat and betray in what they complacently assumed was a good cause because they espoused it. ...

Those who cultivate and spread the gospel of hatred throughout our society bear a heavy responsibility. They do not really weaken Communism; they weaken democracy and liberty. By their conduct and their philosophy they lower the moral standards of the society they pretend to defend. Eager to put down imagined subversion, they are themselves the most subversive of all the elements in our society, for they subvert "that harmony and affection" without which a society cannot be a commonwealth.

Much of our current foreign policy takes once again the form of indulgence in a double standard of morality.

THE BLACKHORSE PRAYER

GOD, our heavenly Father, hear our prayer. We acknowledge our shortcomings and ask thy help in being better soldiers for thee. Grant us, O Lord, those things we need to do thy work more effectively. Give us this day a gun that will fire 10,000 rounds a second, a napalm which will burn for a week. Help us to bring death and destruction wherever we go, for we do it in thy name and therefore it is meet and just. We thank thee for this war fully mindful that while it is not the best of all wars, it is better than no war at all. We remember that Christ said, "I came not to send peace, but a sword," and we pledge ourselves in all our works to be like Him. Forget not the least of thy children as they hide from us in the jungles; bring them under our merciful hand that we may end their suffering. In all things, O God, assist us, for we do our noble work in the knowledge that only with thy help can we avoid the catastrophe of peace which threatens us ever. All of which we ask in the name of thy son, George Patton. Amen.

Composed by Dr. Livingston and distributed by him at ceremonies for Col. George S. Patton, III in Vietnam.

Thus it is contrary to international law to make reconnaissance flights over the territory of another nation — the Soviet reminded us of that a few years back — but we make such flights over Cuba and China: if Cuban planes flew over Florida or Chinese over Hawaii we might take a less easygoing view of the matter. We justly condemn Nazi destruction of Rotterdam and Warsaw, cities that were not military objectives, but we conveniently forget that we were chiefly responsible for the senseless destruction of Dresden — not a military object — within a few weeks of the end of the war, with a loss of 135,000 lives. It is a matter for rejoicing that we have the nuclear bomb, but when China detonated her first bomb our President told us that "this is a dark day in history." Perhaps so, though so far we are the only nation that has ever used the bomb — a fact which the Asians remember a bit better than we do. And even now Senator Russell assures us that he would favor using it again if our soldiers in Viet-

'National Security' Blanket

nam got into trouble. Even the present war in Vietnam —
the President has now used the word *war* for it, so perhaps
we can abandon the hypocritical vocabulary with which we
have heretofore bemused ourselves — tempts us constantly
to indulge in a double standard. The Vietcong engages in
"terror attacks" but our bombings do not presumably hurt
anybody. When we use gas it is not really gas but just
something our own police use here at home. Our airmen
and marines are "observers" but the enemy's soldiers are
terrorists. Guerrilla warfare — is it from the North? —
justifies bombing at the source: if Castro accepted that
theory and bombed those bases in Florida and Guatemala
that launched guerrilla attacks on his island, we might

30

take a different view of the matter. When the Russians announced that they would not tolerate an unfriendly government in Hungary, and sent their troops and tanks crashing into that country in 1956, we were rightly outraged, but we think it quite right for us to announce that we will not tolerate an unfriendly regime in Santo Domingo and to send 20,000 Marines to "restore order" in that island. We complain, and rightly, that other countries do not abide by their international agreements, but we are ready to forgive ourselves for brushing aside international agreements when we face something we regard as an "emergency."

We have always criticized secret diplomacy — remember President Wilson's crusade — but when the CIA operates with such secrecy that even our own government is apparently taken by surprise, that just shows how clever we are. For the Russians or the Chinese to stir up revolution in other lands is subversive of international order, but when we encourage a coup d'etat or a revolution — from Iran to Brazil to Vietnam — it is all in a good cause.

We have not of late heard quite so much as some months back of what must surely be counted the ultimate arrogance — the cry of the "better dead than Red" crusaders. Those highly vocal martyrs are so sure that they are quite ready to condemn to extinction not only themselves and their fellow citizens, but the rest of the world and all potential posterity.

It is three-quarters of a century now since Lord Acton made the famous pronouncement that all power tends to corrupt and that absolute power corrupts absolutely. We had thought, and hoped, that we were exempt from this rule, but it is clear that we are not. Power exposes us to the same temptation to ruthlessness, lawlessness, hypocrisy, and vanity to which all great powers were exposed in the past.

In a simpler day we could survive this threat of corruption without serious damage. We could count on wearing out the brief spell of violence and corruption, or on circumscribing its effects. But now that we are a world power and our conduct affects the fate of every nation on the globe, we can no longer afford this piece of self-indulgence. Now we must square our conduct with principles of law and of morality that will withstand the scrutiny of public opinion everywhere and the tests of history as well.

31

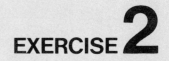

ABILITY TO DISCRIMINATE

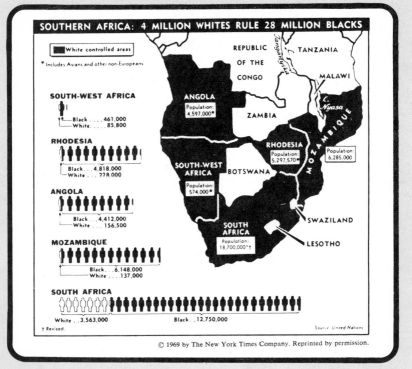

SOUTHERN AFRICA: 4 MILLION WHITES RULE 28 MILLION BLACKS

White controlled areas

* Includes Asians and other non-Europeans

SOUTH-WEST AFRICA
Black 461,000
White 85,800

RHODESIA
Black . . . 4,818,000
White . . . 278,000

ANGOLA
Black . . . 4,412,000
White . . . 156,500

MOZAMBIQUE
Black . . . 6,148,000
White . . . 137,000

SOUTH AFRICA
White . . 3,563,000   Black . . 12,750,000
† Revised.

REPUBLIC OF THE CONGO   TANZANIA   MALAWI

ANGOLA Population: 4,597,000*   ZAMBIA

RHODESIA Population: 5,297,570*   MOZAMBIQUE Population: 6,285,000

SOUTH-WEST AFRICA Population: 574,000*   BOTSWANA

SOUTH AFRICA Population: 18,700,000*†   SWAZILAND   LESOTHO

Source: United Nations

© 1969 by The New York Times Company. Reprinted by permission.

Usually difficult situations fail to present easy choices. Real life problems are too complex to permit simple choices between absolute right and wrong. The following exercise will test your ability to discriminate between degrees of truth and falsehood by completing the questionnaire. Circle the number on the continuum which most closely identifies your evaluation of each statement about South Africa.

1. The white government of South Africa maintains a strict policy of racial separation called Apartheid.

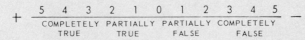

+   5   4   3   2   1   0   1   2   3   4   5   –

COMPLETELY   PARTIALLY   PARTIALLY   COMPLETELY
   TRUE   TRUE   FALSE   FALSE

2. Racial segregation and discrimination in South Africa is similar to the situation one finds in the state of Mississippi today.

+ | 5 | 4 | 3 | 2 | 1 | 0 | 1 | 2 | 3 | 4 | 5 | —
COMPLETELY TRUE   PARTIALLY TRUE   PARTIALLY FALSE   COMPLETELY FALSE

3. Racial discrimination practiced in South Africa is more severe than in any region of the U. S.

+ | 5 | 4 | 3 | 2 | 1 | 0 | 1 | 2 | 3 | 4 | 5 | —
COMPLETELY TRUE   PARTIALLY TRUE   PARTIALLY FALSE   COMPLETELY FALSE

4. Because of South Africa's racist policies, the U. S. should break diplomatic relations with that country.

+ | 5 | 4 | 3 | 2 | 1 | 0 | 1 | 2 | 3 | 4 | 5 | —
COMPLETELY TRUE   PARTIALLY TRUE   PARTIALLY FALSE   COMPLETELY FALSE

5. American statesmen periodically make strong speeches denouncing South African Apartheid, but speeches are not action. Our government continues to support American business investments in South Africa that return handsome profits.

+ | 5 | 4 | 3 | 2 | 1 | 0 | 1 | 2 | 3 | 4 | 5 | —
COMPLETELY TRUE   PARTIALLY TRUE   PARTIALLY FALSE   COMPLETELY FALSE

6. It is hypocritical for the U. S. Government to fight what it considers communist aggression in one part of the world, while at the same time it cooperates politically and economically with a white supremist South African government that commits aggression against its colored majority every day.

+ | 5 | 4 | 3 | 2 | 1 | 0 | 1 | 2 | 3 | 4 | 5 | —
COMPLETELY TRUE   PARTIALLY TRUE   PARTIALLY FALSE   COMPLETELY FALSE

7. Normal diplomatic relations with South Africa are fitting and proper. Political and economic relations with that country does not imply approval of its domestic policies. It only recognizes the fact that the white supremist government is in control.

+ | 5 | 4 | 3 | 2 | 1 | 0 | 1 | 2 | 3 | 4 | 5 | —
COMPLETELY TRUE   PARTIALLY TRUE   PARTIALLY FALSE   COMPLETELY FALSE

AMERICA'S ROLE IN THE WORLD

by Richard M. Nixon*

(Richard M. Nixon has served as president of the United States since January, 1969. The first of the following two readings by President Nixon was presented to Congress on February 18, 1970, and the second reading is a speech he delivered at commencement exercises at the Air Force Academy, Colorado Springs, Colorado, on June 4, 1969.)

Bring the following questions to your reading:

1. What three conditions does President Nixon feel are necessary for a durable peace?
2. What is the central thesis of the "Nixon Doctrine"?
3. What is the first objective of our foreign policy in the president's estimation?

Department of State Bulletin, March 9, 1970, pp. 274-79 and June 23, 1969, pp. 525-28. For a more comprehensive picture of the Nixon administration's foreign policy see *U.S. Foreign Policy for the 1970's: Building for Peace,* available from the Superintendent of Documents, U.S. Government Printing Office, Washington, D.C. 20402. This 235 page book, which costs $1.00, contains President Nixon's foreign policy report to Congress on February 25, 1971.

In the first postwar decades, American energies were absorbed in coping with a cycle of recurrent crises, whose fundamental origins lay in the destruction of World War II and the tensions attending the emergence of scores of new nations. Our opportunity today — and challenge — is to get at the causes of crises, to take a longer view, and to help build the international relationships that will provide the framework of a durable peace.

I have often reflected on the meaning of "peace," and have reached one certain conclusion: Peace must be far more than the absence of war. Peace must provide a durable structure of international relationships which inhibits or removes the causes of war. Building a lasting peace requires a foreign policy guided by three basic principles:

—Peace requires *partnership.* Its obligations, like its benefits, must be shared. This concept of partnership guides our relations with all friendly nations.

—Peace requires *strength.* So long as there are those who would threaten our vital interests and those of our allies with military force, we must be strong. American weakness could tempt would-be aggressors to make dangerous miscalculations. At the same time, our own strength is important only in relation to the strength of others. We — like others — must place high priority on enhancing our security through cooperative arms control.

—Peace requires a *willingness to negotiate.* All nations — and we are no exception — have important national interests to protect. But the most fundamental interest of all nations lies in building the structure of peace. In partnership with our allies, secure in our own strength, we will seek those areas in which we can agree among ourselves and with others to accommodate conflicts and overcome rivalries. We are working toward the day when *all* nations will have a stake in peace, and will therefore be partners in its maintenance. ...

1. PEACE THROUGH PARTNERSHIP — THE NIXON DOCTRINE

This is the message of the doctrine I announced at Guam — the "Nixon Doctrine." Its central thesis is that the United States will participate in the defense and development of allies and friends, but that America cannot — and will not — conceive *all* the plans, design *all* the programs, execute *all* the decisions and undertake *all* the

35

defense of the free nations of the world. We will help where it makes a real difference and is considered in our interest. ...

Our objective, in the first instance, is to support our *interests* over the long run with a sound foreign policy. The more that policy is based on a realistic assessment of our and others' interests, the more effective our role in the world can be. We are not involved in the world because we have commitments; we have commitments because we are involved. Our interests must shape our commitments, rather than the other way around. ...

—In Europe, our policies embody precisely the three principles of a durable peace: partnership, continued strength to defend our common interests when challenged, and willingness to negotiate differences with adversaries.

—Here in the Western Hemisphere we seek to strengthen our special relationship with our sister republics through a new program of action for progress in which all voices are heard and none predominates.

—In Asia, where the Nixon Doctrine was enunciated, partnership will have special meaning for our policies — as evidenced by our strengthened ties with Japan. Our cooperation with Asian nations will be enhanced as they cooperate with one another and develop regional institutions.

—In Vietnam, we seek a just settlement which all parties to the conflict, and all Americans, can support. We are working closely with the South Vietnamese to strengthen their ability to defend themselves. As South Vietnam grows stronger, the other side will, we hope, soon realize that it becomes ever more in their interest to negotiate a just peace.

—In the Middle East, we shall continue to work with others to establish a possible framework within which the parties to the Arab-Israeli conflict can negotiate the complicated and difficult questions at issue. Others must join us in recognizing that a settlement will require sacrifices and restraints by all concerned.

—Africa, with its historic ties to so many of our own citizens, must always retain a significant place in our partnership with the new nations. Africans will play the major role in fulfilling their just aspirations — an end to racialism, the building of new nations, freedom from outside interference, and cooperative economic development. But we will add our efforts to theirs to help realize Africa's great potential.

—In an ever more interdependent world economy, American foreign policy will emphasize the freer flow of capital and goods between nations. ...

2. AMERICA'S STRENGTH

The second element of a durable peace must be America's strength. Peace, we have learned, cannot be gained by good will alone.

In determining the strength of our defenses, we must make precise and crucial judgments. We should spend no more than is necessary. But there is an irreducible minimum of essential military security: for if we are less strong than necessary, and if the worst happens, there will be no domestic society to look after. The magnitude of such a catastrophe, and the reality of the opposing military power that could threaten it, present a risk which requires of any President the most searching and careful attention to the state of our defenses. ...

This Administration has established procedures for the intensive scrutiny of defense issues in the light of overall national priorities. We have re-examined our strategic forces; we have reassessed our general purpose forces; and we have engaged in the most painstaking preparation ever undertaken by the United States Government for arms control negotiations.

3. WILLINGNESS TO NEGOTIATE — AN ERA OF NEGOTIATION

Partnership and strength are two of the pillars of the structure of a durable peace. Negotiation is the third. For our commitment to peace is most convincingly demonstrated in our willingness to negotiate our points of difference in a fair and businesslike manner with the Communist countries.

We are under no illusions. We know that there are enduring ideological differences. We are aware of the difficulty in moderating tensions that arise from the clash of national interests. These differences will not be dissipated by changes of atmosphere or dissolved in

37

cordial personal relations between statesmen. They involve strong convictions and contrary philosophies, necessities of national security, and the deep-seated differences of perspectives formed by geography and history.

The United States, like any other nation, has interests of its own, and will defend those interests. But any nation today must define its interests with special concern for the interests of others. If some nations define their security in a manner that means insecurity for other nations, then peace is threatened and the security of all is diminished. This obligation is particularly great for the nuclear super-powers on whose decisions the survival of mankind may well depend.

U.S. IS COMMITTED TO WORLD FREEDOM

The cause of freedom has been the central commitment of our nation since its birth. It is the central issue in the world struggle in which we are engaged. The first purpose of our foreign policy, and of the military power which supports it, is to defend freedom — without war, if possible. Our foreign policy is designed also to strengthen freedom wherever it exists and to promote it by peaceful means where it is still suppressed.

Secretary of State Dean Rusk at Barnard College, January 22, 1964.

The United States is confident that tensions can be eased and the danger of war reduced by patient and precise efforts to reconcile conflicting interests on concrete issues. Coexistence demands more than a spirit of good will. It requires the definition of positive goals which can be sought and achieved cooperatively. It requires real progress toward resolution of specific differences. This is our objective.

THE STRUCTURE OF PEACE

For the past four years this Nation has engaged in patient and prolonged diplomacy in every corner of the world, and we have also maintained the strength that has made our diplomacy credible and peace possible. As a result, we are well on the way toward erecting what I have often referred to as a structure of peace, a structure that rests on the hard concrete of common interests and mutual agreements, and not on the shifting sands of naive sentimentality. ...

In the past four years, my efforts to build that structure of peace have taken me to 22 countries, including four world capitals never visited by an American President before — Peking, Moscow, Warsaw, and Bucharest. Everywhere I have traveled I have seen evidence that the times are on the side of peace, if America maintains its strength and continues on course. ...

Throughout the world today America is respected. This is partly because we have entered a new era of initiative in American foreign policy and the world's leaders and its people have seen the results. But it is also because the world has come to know America. It knows we are a nation of peaceful intentions, of honorable purposes, true to our commitments. We are respected because for a third of a century under six Presidents we have met the responsibilities of a great and free nation. We have not retreated from the world. We have not betrayed our allies.

Address to the nation by President Nixon on November 4, 1972.

Reflect on the following questions while you read:

1. How does President Nixon feel about unilateral disarmament by the United States?
2. President Nixon claims ''we stand at a crossroad in our history.'' What does he mean by this statement?
3. What comments does the president make about spending for defense?

What is America's role in the world? What are the responsibilities of a great nation toward protecting freedom beyond its shores? Can we ever be left in peace if we do not actively assume the burden of keeping the peace?

When great questions are posed, fundamental differences of opinion come into focus. It serves no purpose to gloss over these differences or to try to pretend that they are mere matters of degree.

Because there is one school of thought that holds that the road to understanding with the Soviet Union and Communist China lies through a downgrading of our own alliances and what amounts to a unilateral reduction of our own arms — in order to demonstrate our "good faith."

They believe that we can be conciliatory and accommodating only if we do not have the strength to be otherwise. They believe America will be able to deal with the possibility of peace only when we are unable to cope with the threat of war.

Those who think that way have grown weary of the weight of free-world leadership that fell upon us in the wake of World War II. They argue that we, the United States, are as much responsible for the tensions in the world as the adversaries we face.

They assert that the United States is blocking the road to peace by maintaining its military strength at home and its defenses abroad. If we would only reduce our forces, they contend, tensions would disappear and the chances for peace would brighten. America's powerful military presence on the world scene, they believe, makes peace abroad improbable and peace at home impossible.

Now, we should never underestimate the appeal of the isolationist school of thought. Their slogans are simplistic and powerful: "Charity begins at home. Let's first solve our problems at home and then we can deal with the problems of the world."

This simple formula touches a responsive chord with many an overburdened taxpayer. It would be easy, easy for the President of the United States to buy some popularity by going along with the new isolationists. But I submit to you that it would be disastrous for our nation and the world.

THE DIRECTION AMERICA MUST TAKE

I hold a totally different view of the world, and I come to a different conclusion about the direction America must take.

Imagine for a moment, if you will, what would happen to this world if America were to become a dropout in assuming the responsibility for defending peace and freedom in the world. As every world leader knows and as even the most outspoken critics of America would admit, the rest of the world would live in terror.

Because if America were to turn its back on the world, there would be peace that would settle over this planet, but it would be the kind of peace that suffocated freedom in Czechoslovakia.

The danger to us has changed, but it has not vanished. We must revitalize our alliances, not abandon them.

We must rule out unilateral disarmament, because in the real world it wouldn't work. If we pursue arms control as an end in itself, we will not achieve our end. The adversaries in the world are not in conflict because they are armed. They are armed because they are in conflict and have not yet learned peaceful ways to resolve their conflicting national interests.

The aggressors of this world are not going to give the United States a period of grace in which to put our domestic house in order, just as the crises within our society cannot be put on a back burner until we resolve the problem of Viet-Nam.

The most successful solutions that we can possibly imagine for our domestic programs will be meaningless if we are not around to enjoy them. Nor can we conduct a successful peace policy abroad if our society is at war with itself at home.

There is no advancement for Americans at home in a retreat from the problems of the world. I say that America has a vital national interest in world stability, and no other nation can uphold that interest for us.

We stand at a crossroad in our history. We shall reaffirm our destiny for greatness, or we shall choose instead to withdraw into ourselves. The choice will affect far more than our foreign policy; it will determine the quality of our lives.

41

A nation needs many qualities, but it needs faith and confidence above all. Skeptics do not build societies; the idealists are the builders. Only societies that believe in themselves can rise to their challenges. Let us not, then, pose a false choice between meeting our responsibilities abroad and meeting the needs of our people at home. We shall meet both or we shall meet neither. ...

RESURGENCE OF AMERICAN IDEALISM

We will know then that every man achieves his own greatness by reaching out beyond himself, and so it is with nations. When a nation believes in itself — as Athenians did in their Golden Age, as Italians did in the Renaissance — that nation can perform miracles. Only when a nation means something to itself can it mean something to others.

That is why I believe a resurgence of American idealism can bring about a modern miracle — and that modern miracle is a world order of peace and justice. ...

However, I must warn you that in the years to come you may hear your commitment to the American responsibility in the world derided as a form of militarism. It is important that you recognize that strawman issue for what it is: the outward sign of a desire by some to turn America inward and to have America turn away from greatness. ...

NEED FOR NATIONAL SECURITY

The American defense establishment should never be a sacred cow, but on the other hand, the American military should never be anybody's scapegoat. ...

"WE MUST NOT CONFUSE OUR PRIORITIES"

There can be no question that we should not spend unnecessarily for defense. But we must also not confuse our priorities.

The question, I submit, in defense spending is a very simple one: "How much is necessary?" The President of the United States is the man charged with making that judgment. ...

Mistakes in military policy today can be irretrievable.

Time lost in this age of science can never be regained. America had months in order to prepare and to catch up in order to wage World War I. We had months and even years in order to catch up so we could play a role in winning World War II. When a war can be decided in 20 minutes, the nation that is behind will have no time to catch up.

I say: Let America never fall behind in maintaining the defenses necessary for the strength of this nation.

I have no choice in my decisions but to come down on the side of security, because history has dealt harshly with those nations who have taken the other course. ...

THE NEW
AMERICAN MILITARISM

by Colonel James A. Donovan*

(Colonel James A. Donovan joined the Marines following his graduation from Dartmouth College. Decorated with the Silver Star and Bronze Star medals, Colonel Donovan served as an infantry officer in World War II and in Korea, where he was an analyst of Marine operations for the Commander in Chief, Pacific. He attended the Industrial College of the Armed Forces and served as a staff planner on the general staff at Marine Headquarters.  After retirement from the Corps in 1963, he became president and publisher of the 100-year old *Journal of the Armed Forces.* Since 1967 Colonel Donovan has worked as a free-lance writer and researcher.)

The following questions should help your understanding of the reading:

1. What is the basic theme of Colonel Donovan's reading?
2. What does Colonel Donovan feel are some of the reasons for America's excessive military influence in planning and carrying out our country's foreign policy?

*James A. Donovan, *Militarism, U.S.A.* (New York: Charles Scribner's Sons, 1970), pp. 1-3, 16, 23, 24. Reprinted by permission of Charles Scribner's Sons from *Militarism, U.S.A.* by James A. Donovan. Copyright © 1970 James A. Donovan.

America has become a militaristic and aggressive nation embodied in a vast, expensive, and burgeoning military-industrial-scientific-political combine which dominates the country and effects much of our daily life, our economy, our international status, and our foreign policies.

Through most of its history, America has had a tradition which rejected militarism except under the pressures of a nationally declared general war. Now, however, there is impressive evidence that the United States is moving inexorably toward a society that is increasingly influenced by the defense establishment. Moreover, this is happening not as a result of a deliberate choice by the American people, but as a result of an accumulation of military decisions, and actions that are beyond the control of present democratic processes. ...

The American people have ... become more and more accustomed to militarism, to uniforms, to the cult of the gun, and to the violence of combat. Whole generations have been brought up on war news and wartime propaganda; the few years of peace since 1939 have seen a steady stream of war novels, war movies, comic strips, and television programs with war or military settings. To many Americans, military training, expeditionary service, and warfare are merely extensions of the entertainment and games of childhood.

General David M. Shoup, former Commandant of the U.S. Marine Corps.

American armed might is on frontier guard duty; patrolling the air and seas, or stationed on foreign shores around the world. It has been conducting an undeclared war for five years at a cost of 40,000 American dead, over 260,000 wounded and $104 billion spent, in a small underdeveloped country 8,400 miles from U.S. shores. In addition to the 600,000 military men in Southeast Asia, there are 300,000 U.S. Ground and Air Forces stationed in Europe and South Korea. Tens of thousands of Americans serve in warships on the high seas. There are over 1,200,000

U.S. fighting men stationed overseas at 2,270 locations in 119 countries. Additional divisions, air forces, and fleets stand by in the continental United States prepared to execute numerous contingency plans for every area in the world deemed to be of interest to the defense and welfare of the United States and its allies. ...

The nation's armed forces are supported by a vast and permanent arms industry and a complex of related interests which affect thousands of communities and millions of citizens. These Americans — in uniform, veterans of military service, defense-industry employees and their dependents, defense scientists, Defense Department civilians, businessmen, and politicians — all have

Pierotti in the New York Post

"Yes, this is the White House, the State Department, the Senate, and the House. Which do you want?"

direct and personal interests in the nature and scope of militarism and the activities of the defense establishment. ...

Our military power ostensibly has been intended only to defend the nation and to help protect its friends and its allies from attack, yet it has become the cause of much national dissension and disagreement. It is the reason for a good deal of American unpopularity abroad. Our military power has come to be viewed by many people as a self-perpetuating force of aggression and destruction motivated by many interests beyond the needs of national defense. ...

It was during ... early post-World War II years that distinguished wartime military leaders shifted to influential policy-making and leadership positions throughout the government, diplomatic, and business sectors. The victorious American generals and admirals enjoyed world-wide respect, their countrymen were deeply proud of their accomplishments, and they were widely recognized as leaders, planners, and managers. Because of accelerated wartime promotions some were retiring from military careers at an early age. Many were available for further useful service and were sought out by government and industry. The extent of military penetration into the civilian hierarchy after World War II was without precedent in American history. ...

THE DANGER OF A LARGE MILITARY ESTABLISHMENT

How many of you realize that just before World War II the entire American Army, including the Air Corps, numbered 139,000 men?

Now we have three and a half million men under arms. ...

As long as we keep that big an army, it will always find things to do. If the Vietnam War stopped tomorrow, the chances are that with that big a military establishment we would be in another such adventure, abroad or at home, before you knew it.

George Wald, a Nobel Prize winner and Professor of Biology at Harvard.

The basis of America's modern militarism has been a hallowed trinity of ideals or creeds; *patriotism, national defense,* and *anti-Communism.* These terms mean different things to different people and each can be employed to motivate and justify actions, to attack opposing ideas, and as a refuge for the chauvinist. Their pure and simple meanings are not in themselves a basis for militarism but they are frequently used and distorted by militarists for many purposes. Like "motherhood," "hot dogs," and the "Fourth of July" these terms are all-American, sacrosanct, and usually held above criticism. American militarism is founded upon this trinity of ideological beliefs which are the source of the national military policy — but American militarism is *motivated* by much less well recognized factors; defense-establishment careerism, defense-industry profits, fascination with military technology and weapons of destruction — and a national pride and competitive spirit. It is also prompted by the many alliances and commitments we have assumed to safeguard the "Free World."

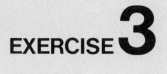

EVALUATING SOURCES

A critical thinker must always question his various sources of information. Historians, for example, usually distinguish between *primary sources* (eyewitness accounts) and *secondary sources* (writings based on primary or eyewitness accounts, or other secondary sources). Most textbooks are examples of secondary sources. A diary written by a Civil War veteran is one example of a primary source. In order to be a critical reader one must be able to recognize primary sources. However, this is not enough. Eyewitness accounts do not always provide accurate descriptions. Historians may find ten different eyewitness accounts of an event and all the accounts might interpret the event differently. Then they must decide which of these accounts provide the most objective and accurate interpretations.

Test your skill in evaluating sources by participating in the following exercise. Pretend you are living 2000 years in the future. Your teacher tells you to write an essay about the causes of conflict in the Middle East during the 20th century. Consider carefully each of the following source descriptions. First, *underline* only those descriptions you feel would serve as a primary source for your essay. Second, *rank* only the underlined or primary sources assigning the number (1) to the most objective and accurate primary source, number (2) to the next most accurate and so on until the ranking is finished. Then discuss and compare your evaluations with other class members.

Assume that all of the following individuals all wrote essays, articles, and books dealing with the broad problem of conflict in the Middle East.

1. Yassir Arafat, a leader of Palestine liberation forces

2. President Richard Nixon

3. Premier Golda Meir of Israel

4. A Japanese journalist

5. Prime Minister Indira Ghandi of India

6. President Anwar Sadat of Egypt

7. Premier Fidel Castro of Cuba

8. David Ben Gurion, former Premier of Israel

9. Governor George Wallace

10. Gamal Abdul Nasser, former president of Egypt

11. President Thieu of South Vietnam

12. General Moshe Dayan of Israel

13. Premier Alexei Kosygin of Russia

14. Chairman Mao Tse Tung of Communist China

15. President John F. Kennedy

THE PROBLEM
OF
COMMUNISM

Readings:
1. The Menace of Communism
      Strom Thurmond
2. Old Myths and New Realities
      J. W. Fulbright

THE MENACE OF COMMUNISM

by Strom Thurmond*

(Strom Thurmond has been a United States Senator from South Carolina since 1965. He was formerly a lawyer who was the recipient of many medals during the second world war. He is also active in such organizations as The American Legion, Veterans of Foreign Wars and Sons of the American Revolution.)

The following questions should help your understanding of the reading:

1. Why does Senator Thurmond believe that the international communist movement does not lack unity?
2. What proof does the author give to support his claim that American radical groups, in particular the Black Panthers, are working with the communist movement?
3. What does Senator Thurmond feel is the "key element" in communist strategy today?
4. According to Senator Thurmond, what international goals were agreed to at an international meeting of communists in Moscow?

*Senator Strom Thurmond before the United States Senate on November 13, 1969.

We must recognize that times have changed and our understanding of the Communist movement must change with the times. In my view, the Communists are doing a good job of adapting to changed conditions so that their movement can have a more powerful effect and be much more solidly established throughout the world. ...

The keystone of these international activities was the World Conference of Communist and Workers' Parties held in Moscow last June. This meeting deserves close scrutiny, since it laid down Communist policy for their followers all over the world. It was an entirely new event. No such meeting had ever taken place before. It is the modern substitute for the old Comintern, or Communist International, providing central coordination and direction. Those who think that the Communist movement lacks unity need to take these meetings seriously. I do not have the time to go into a full study of the meeting, but I have studied the speech of Gus Hall, general secretary of the Communist Party U.S.A.

COEXISTENCE IS IMPOSSIBLE

We are living not merely in a state but in a system of states, and the existence of the Soviet Republic side by side with imperialist states for a long time is unthinkable. One or the other must triumph in the end. And before this end supervenes, a series of frightful collisions between the Soviet Republic and the bourgeoise states will be inevitable.

Lenin at the Eighth Congress of the Communist Party in 1919.

Gus Hall was made general secretary in 1960. This date coincides with the opening of the new assault by the Communists to infiltrate and manipulate the youth movement in the United States. Today we are witnessing the fruit of of Gus Hall's efforts. Although some choose to treat the Moscow-controlled Communist Party as a group of tired old men, no longer radical enough to appeal to youth, Gus Hall knows different. He was a young Communist himself in the thirties. He knows how the discipline of the Moscow Communists outlasts the emotional radicalism of some revolutionaries. He knows how to direct and control the wild excesses of those who claim to be "to the left" of the CPUSA. His speech at the world conference in June laid down the line which even those who profess to be independent are following.

Before I go into detailed analysis of this speech, I would like to cite just one example. The Black Panthers are supposed to be a violent revolutionary group out of harmony with the supposedly stodgy doctrine of the Moscow Communists. Yet the Black Panthers have their little role to play in the Moscow-directed drama.

A short while ago, a number of Senators discussed on the floor of the Senate the activities of William Kunstler, attorney for Dave Dellinger and the "conspiracy 8," in negotiating with Hanoi to get information about Americans held as prisoners of war by North Korea. Kunstler returned from Paris and reported that American relatives would have to work with the Communist-dominated New Mobilization Committee — the very committee organizing the current mobilization — to obtain information about their loved ones.

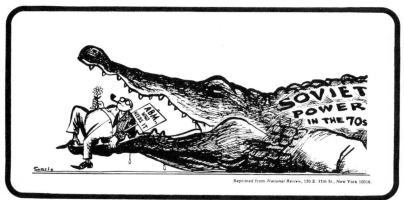

Reprinted from *National Review*, 150 E. 35th St., New York 10016.

This was shocking enough. However, few even now realize that the same group of individuals — Kunstler, Dellinger, and representatives of the Hanoi regime — are also trying to engineer a so-called "exchange of prisoners." Their idea of such an exchange is to trade Americans held in Hanoi for Black Panthers held in American jails for such common crimes as murder, incitement to riot, and assault. Whether or not such a "prisoner exchange" could be arranged is beside the point. From the perspective of propaganda, such efforts seek to place guerrilla warfare in Vietnam in the same category as guerrilla warfare in the United States.

In other words, those who become entangled in such byplay are actually drawn into supporting those in the

United States who advocate the violent overthrow of the Government of the United States.

In the same way, the multiple goals of the international Communist movement are too complex to be studied in isolation. Thus thousands of people are being "mobilized" with little understanding of the ultimate ends they serve.

Such people think that they can promote their own activities without reference to the backdrop of the world around them. They think that a narrow-minded interest in "peace" will actually serve to establish harmony and friendship between nations.

Modern propaganda no longer seeks to change the minds of the people upon which the propaganda is designed to have influence. The object of propaganda is to move people toward precontrived goals without those affected realizing that they are moving toward those goals. This is a key element in the Communist strategy today. Instead of trying to convert millions of people to Marxist-Leninist ideology, the Communists seek to mobilize the people toward the specific goals of the current strategy rather than to the long-range doctrines of the classic revolutionists.

The so-called peace demonstrations being organized here this week fit into the pattern of propaganda designed to mobilize masses of people. The Vietnam war is only one element of a program of total conflict carried on at all levels between the Communist system and the free world. The Communist strategy of war has moved beyond fighting on the battlefield. Such fighting is only one tool, one weapon, in the Communist assault. In addition to the war in Vietnam, one must consider the relationship between the Soviet Union and the United States, the changed balance of strategic nuclear power, the rising tide of Soviet naval strength, the Soviet program of wars of liberation in many areas of the world, including the Middle East. These goals were articulated at the World Conference of Communist and Worker's Parties held in Moscow last June.

The goals of the Moscow conference were summarized in an official lengthy document containing nine points approved by the delegates. I will mention each of these briefly:

First. The Communists called for united action to support the heroic Vietnamese people and welcomed the formation of the Revolutionary Provisional Government of South Vietnam.

THE MYTH OF PEACEFUL COEXISTENCE

I wish I could confirm that the so-called detente, about which we have heard so much, actually exists, and that the residual differences with the Soviet Union are being progressively reduced by a growing community of interests.

Unfortunately, I can give you no such rosy estimate of the state of world affairs.

Wherever one looks, whether to Southeast Asia, or the Mideast, or Africa, or Latin America, all evidence indicates that the Cold War is intensifying; that the coming period will confront our nation and the other free nations with the cruelest test of perseverance and courage and of the will to survive.

I know that there are many people who do believe in the existence of the detente, and that the theory has even received some support from official sources.

But I find it difficult to understand how anyone who examines the history of the past decade, especially the history of the past five years, could read this meaning into the course of events.

It makes no sense to talk about a detente in a decade that has witnessed the suppression of the Hungarian revolution, the rape of Tibet, the Communist seizure of Cuba, the Cuban missile crisis, the Soviet violation of the moratorium on nuclear testing, the establishment of puppet Communist dictatorships in the Brazzaville Congo and in Zanzibar, and two Communist attempts to seize power in the Congo.

Nor does it make sense to talk about a detente in a period that has witnessed two Communist attacks of India, the war in Vietnam, growing Communist insurgencies in Thailand and Laos, the launching of half a dozen guerrilla movements in the countries of the Americas, the attempted Communist take-over in the Dominican Republic, and the recent war in the Middle East. ...

> Most Americans are agreed, I believe, on the need to stand up against the danger of Soviet expansion in the Middle East and to support Israel against Arab extremists. Unfortunately, however, our people are divided in their support of our Vietnam commitments. Many of those who understand the importance of holding the line in the Middle East apparently do not understand the importance of holding the line in the Far East.
>
> They fail to realize that these two conflicts are part of a larger global conflict between the forces of freedom and the forces of Communist slavery.

Senator Thomas Dodd of Connecticut before the Senate, February 26, 1968.

Second. They proclaimed that the main link of united action remains the antiwar struggle.

Third. They claimed that the defense of peace is inseparably linked up with compelling imperialists to accept peaceful coexistence.

Fourth. They called upon all delegates to intensify the struggle against militarism of all forms, especially against the so-called military-industrial complex of the United States.

Fifth. They demanded the seating of Communist China in the U.N. and the handing over of Taiwan to the Peking regime.

Sixth. They demanded the elimination of the vestiges of colonialism in South Africa, Mozambique, and similar areas.

Seventh. They called upon their members to step up the fight against the Fascist menace in Greece, Spain, Portugal, West Germany, and elsewhere.

Eighth. They called upon the delegates to be united against racialism.

Ninth. They called upon the delegates to defend and win the right of freedom of speech and to release those languishing in jails.

This is the agenda of Communist agitators the world over. These issues are being exploited here in an attempt to weaken the power and influence of the United States. They are to be used as issues to split the people of the United States and the free world.

OLD MYTHS
AND NEW REALITIES

by J. W. Fulbright*

(J. W. Fulbright is a former member of the House of Representatives and has been a United States Senator since 1945. He has been one of the senate's most outspoken critics of U.S. involvement in Vietnam as chairman of The Senate Foreign Relations Committee. Before serving in Congress he was a professor of law at the University of Arkansas and served as president of the university from 1939-1941.)

Use the following questions to help your understanding of the reading:

1. What evidence does Senator Fulbright present when he suggests that the cold war has mellowed?
2. What does Senator Fulbright mean when he states we Americans are used to looking at the world and ourselves in moralistic rather than empirical terms?
3. What does the Senator mean when he says "we are clinging to old myths in the face of new realities?"

*Senator J. W. Fulbright before the United States Senate on March 25, 1964.

There has always — and inevitably — been some divergence between the realities of foreign policy and our ideas about it. This divergence has in certain respects been growing rather than narrowing and we are handicapped, accordingly, by policies based on old myths rather than current realities. ...

Although it is too soon to render a definitive judgment, there is mounting evidence that events of recent years have wrought profound changes in the character of East-West relations. In the Cuban missile crisis of October 1962, the United States proved to the Soviet Union that a policy of aggression and adventure involved unacceptable risks. In the signing of the test ban treaty each side in effect assured the other that it was prepared to forego, at least for the present, any bid for a decisive military or political breakthrough. These occurrences, it should be added, took place against the background of the clearly understood strategic superiority — but not supremacy — of the United States.

It seems reasonable, therefore, to suggest that the character of the cold war has, for the present at least, been profoundly altered: by the drawing back of the Soviet Union from extremely aggressive policies; by the implicit repudiation by both sides of a policy of "total victory;" and by the establishment of an American strategic superiority which the Soviet Union appears to have tacitly accepted because it has been accompanied by assurances that it will be exercised by the United States with responsibility and restraint. These enormously important changes may come to be regarded by historians as the foremost achievements of the Kennedy Administration in the field of foreign policy. Their effect has been to commit us to a foreign policy which can accurately — though perhaps not prudently — be defined as one of "peaceful co-existence." ...

These astonishing changes in the configuration of the postwar world have had an unsettling effect on both public and official opinion in the United States. One reason for this, I believe, lies in the fact that we are a people used to looking at the world, and indeed at ourselves, in moralistic rather than empirical terms. We are predisposed to regard any conflict as a clash between good and evil rather than as simply a clash between conflicting interests. We are inclined to confuse freedom and democracy, which we regard as moral principles, with the way in which they are practiced in America — with

60

capitalism, federalism, and the two-party system, which are not moral principles but simply the preferred and accepted practices of the American people. There is much cant in American moralism and not a little inconsistency. It resembles in some ways the religious faith of the many respectable people who, in Samuel Butler's words, "would be equally horrified to hear the Christian religion doubted or to see it practiced."

Our national vocabulary is full of "self-evident truths," not only about "life, liberty, and happiness," but about a vast number of personal and public issues, including the cold war. It has become one of the "self-evident truths" of the postwar era that just as the President resides in Washington and the Pope in Rome, the Devil resides immutably in Moscow. ...

We are confronted with a complex and fluid world situation and we are not adapting ourselves to it. We are clinging to old myths in the face of new realities and we are seeking to escape the contradictions by narrowing the permissible bounds of public discussion, by relegating an increasing number of ideas and viewpoints to a growing category of "unthinkable thoughts." I believe that this tendency can and should be reversed, that it is within our ability, and unquestionably in our interests, to cut loose from established myths and to start thinking some "unthinkable thoughts" — about the cold war and East-West relations, about the under-developed countries and particularly those in Latin America, about the changing nature of the Chinese Communist threat in Asia and about the festering war in Vietnam.

The master myth of the cold war is that the Communist bloc is a monolith composed of governments which are not really governments at all but organized conspiracies, divided among themselves perhaps in certain matters of tactics, but all equally resolute and implacable in their determination to destroy the free world.

I believe that the Communist world is indeed hostile to the free world in its general and long-term intentions but that the existence of this animosity in principle is far less important for our foreign policy than the great variations in its intensity and character both in time and among the individual members of the Communist bloc. ...

For a start, we can acknowledge the fact that the Soviet Union, though still a most formidable adversary, has ceased to be totally and implacably hostile to the

West. It has shown a new willingness to enter mutually advantageous arrangements with the West and, thus far at least, to honor them. It has therefore become possible to divert some of our energies from the prosecution of the cold war to the relaxation of the cold war and to deal with the Soviet Union, for certain purposes, as a normal state with normal and traditional interests.

If we are to do these things effectively, we must distinguish between communism as an ideology and the power and policy of the Soviet state. It is not communism as a doctrine, or communism as it is practiced within the Soviet Union or within any other country, that threatens us. How the Soviet Union organizes its internal life, the gods and doctrines that it worships, are matters for the Soviet Union to determine. It is not Communist dogma as espoused within Russia but Communist imperialism that threatens us and other peoples of the non-Communist world. Insofar as a great nation mobilizes its power and resources for aggressive purposes, that nation, regardless of ideology, makes itself our enemy. Insofar as a nation is content to practice its doctrines within its own frontiers, that nation, however repugnant its ideology, is one with which we have no proper quarrel. We must deal with the Soviet Union as a great power, quite apart from differences of ideology. ...

We are to a great extent the victims, and the Soviets the beneficiaries, of our own ideological convictions, and of the curious contradictions which they involve. We consider it a form of subversion of the free world, for example, when the Russians enter trade relations or conclude a consular convention or establish airline connections with a free country in Asia, Africa, or Latin America — and to a certain extent we are right. On the other hand, when it is proposed that we adopt the same strategy in reverse — by extending commercial credits to Poland or Yugoslavia, or by exchanging ambassadors with a Hungarian regime which has changed considerably in character since the revolution of 1956 — then the same patriots who are so alarmed by Soviet activities in the free world charge our policy makers with ''giving aid and comfort to the enemy'' and with innumerable other categories of idiocy and immorality.

It is time that we resolved this contradiction and separated myth from reality. The myth is that every Communist state is an unmitigated evil and a relentless enemy of the free world; the reality is that some Communist regimes pose a threat to the free world while others pose little or none, and that if we will recognize these distinctions, we ourselves will be able to influence events in the Communist bloc in a way favorable to the security of the free world.

FACT AND OPINION

The cartoon below is one of many recent reactions to American foreign policy. This discussion exercise is designed to promote experimentation with one's ability to distinguish between fact and opinion. It is a fact, for example, that the United States is militarily involved in the Vietnam War. But to say this involvement serves the interests of world peace is an opinion or conclusion. Future historians will agree that American soldiers fought in Vietnam, but their interpretations about the causes and consequences of the war will probably vary greatly.

Snow White and the Seven Experiments

Corky in the Los Angeles Times

Some of the following statements are taken from the two preceding readings and some have other origins. Consider each statement carefully. Mark (O) for any statement you feel is an opinion or interpretation of the facts. Mark (F) for any statement you believe is a fact. Then discuss and compare your judgments with those of other class members.

O = Opinion
F = Fact

____ 1. The United States gives foreign aid only to countries of the free world.

____ 2. The United States gives aid to military dictatorships.

____ 3. The United States gives foreign aid to communist and non-communist countries.

____ 4. The foreign aid budget includes provisions for both economic and military assistance.

____ 5. The master myth of the cold war is that the Communist bloc is a monolith composed of governments which are not really governments at all but organized conspiracies.

____ 6. The communists are still attempting to gain control of non-communist countries.

____ 7. If South Vietnam falls to the communists, the other countries of Indochina will fall one by one.

____ 8. Many Vietnam veterans have testified to war crimes committed in Indochina — not isolated incidents, but crimes committed on a day-to-day basis with the full awareness of officers at all levels of command.

____ 9. The U. S. today maintains a military presence in over 65 foreign countries.

____ 10. North Vietnamese forces infiltrated South Vietnam on a regular basis.

____ 11. American military forces infiltrated South Vietnam on a regular basis.

____ 12. A nation may practice internationalism without having any military forces in foreign lands.

____ 13. Internationalism means the exchange of goods and people, not military power and expansion.

____ 14. Huge military appropriations are needed every year to maintain American security.

CASE STUDY

U.S. - CHINA RELATIONS

In 1971 the United Nations voted to expel Nationalist China after granting Communist China a seat in the General Assembly and on the Security Council (see page 97). The United Nations now recognizes the government in Peking as the official representative of China's people.

President Nixon opened a new door to U.S.-China relations with his visit to Communist China in 1972 (see the following page).

This case study involves a dispute over the nature of Communist China's foreign policy and how the United States should act toward Peking in the future. These questions are of momentous importance. China is the most populated country, containing about one quarter of the world's people (around 800 million). The United States is the richest and most industrialized country, using over half of all the world's resources consumed each year.

There is little hope for peace in Asia or the world unless the people of China and the United States can reach a mutual understanding.

PRESIDENT EXPLAINS HIS CHINA TRIP

The primary goal of this trip was to re-establish communication with the People's Republic of China after a generation of hostility. We achieved that goal. Let me turn now to our joint communique.

We did not bring back any written or unwritten agreements that will guarantee peace in our time. We did not bring home any magic formula which will make unnecessary the efforts of the American people to continue to maintain the strength so that we can continue to be free.

We made some necessary and important beginnings, however, in several areas. We entered into agreements to expand cultural, educational, and journalistic contacts between the Chinese and the American people. We agreed to work to begin and broaden trade between our two countries. We have agreed that the communications that have now been established between our governments will be strengthened and expanded.

Most important, we have agreed on some rules of international conduct which will reduce the risk of confrontation and war in Asia and in the Pacific.

We agreed that we are opposed to domination of the Pacific area by any one power. We agreed that international disputes should be settled without the use of the threat of force and we agreed that we are prepared to apply this principle to our mutual relations.

With respect to Taiwan, we stated our established policy that our forces overseas will be reduced gradually as tensions ease, and that our ultimate objective is to withdraw our forces as a peaceful settlement is achieved.

We have agreed that we will not negotiate the fate of other nations behind their backs, and we did not do so at Peking. There were no secret deals of any kind. We have done all this without giving up any United States commitment to any other country.

In our talks, the talks that I had with the leaders of the People's Republic and that the Secretary of State had with the office of the Government of the People's Republic in the foreign affairs area, we both realized that a bridge of understanding that spans almost 12,000 miles and 22 years of hostility can't be built in 1 week of discussions. But we have agreed to begin to build that bridge, recognizing that our work will require years of patient effort. We made no attempt to pretend that major differences did not exist between our two governments, because they do exist.

Remarks by President Nixon on the day of his return from China, February 28, 1972.

READING NUMBER 9

PEKING'S RECORD
OF GLOBAL AGGRESSION

by Stefan T. Possony*

(Dr. Possony is an Austrian-born author and educator. He is the director of the International Political Studies Program at the Hoover Institution On War, Revolution and Peace at Stanford University, and is an honorary academician of Chinghua Academy in Taipei. He is the author of many books, including *International Relations, Tomorrow's War, Strategic Air Power,* and *Lenin, the Compulsive Revolutionary.*)

Examine these questions before reading Dr. Possony's article:

1. What does the author feel is the main objective of China's foreign policy?
2. How does Dr. Possony describe China's relationship to violent social revolutions in foreign countries?
3. What examples does the author use to support his contention that China is an aggressive nation?

*Stefan T. Possony, "Peking's Record of Global Aggression," *Human Events,* September 4, 1971, pp. 674-75. Reprinted with permission.

In addition to old-fashioned territorial expansion, the main Maoist objective is to implant Maoist regimes in a maximum number of countries. But just as the Soviets did not incorporate Hungary or East Germany into the USSR, so Maoist China does not plan to incorporate India or Afghanistan into the People's Republic of China. Instead, it wishes that the target countries be taken over and ruled by Maoist Communists.

For this purpose they have been using, and clearly intend to use in the future, psychological, economic and political warfare operations and people's wars. Ultimately, if we take Lin Piao at his word, they hope to run such people's wars simultaneously on several continents.

To the extent that their nuclear capabilities grow and become effective, Maoist strategy can be facilitated through blackmail. The Chinese Communist party (CCP) is not a purely political organization like the Communist party of the Soviet Union. Instead, it is an integrated politico-military set-up. The top party leaders have wide military experience, and the top soldiers are holding top party ranks.

All strategic decisions combine political with military strategy. The CCP strategists are not "adventuristic" but prudent, as befits the continuing weakness of China. Neither are they passive. Instead, their strategy is planned for a "protracted" struggle period expected to last from 50 to 100 years.

The use of the People's Liberation Army (PLA) out-side the borders of China is as yet logistically infeasible except in a few contiguous areas. Hence, the Maoists plan to support foreign "liberation" forces but refrain from doing the liberating themselves.

The first step in such a strategy is to establish and enlarge Communist parties in target countries, add sub-ordinate combat organizations, and exercise those in preliminary actions.

To deploy native guerrilla and political forces, the Maoists provide organizational know-how, propaganda support, advisers, training, weapons and small amounts of money. They also enable the local CP's to earn money through the free utilization of printed materials (e.g., magazines) and films, through trade, and through fund collections via the international Maoist network.

"Do I hear a dove down there?"

The second step in the Maoist strategy is to build up bases where the guerrillas can be drilled, deployed and rested. ... Bases in neutral or Communist-controlled countries usually are the best, because the counter-insurgent forces are not normally allowed to cross borders. Bases that are practically inaccessible to the troops of the target country but can be reached by Chinese supply units from the sea are the second best. ...

The third step would be to take advantage of opportunities by provoking and exploiting incidents such as riots and coups, and instigating people's wars in such a way that the Communists who run the operations will be joined by large numbers of "nationalist" and "democratic" freedom fighters. ...

At this writing, regular Chinese forces — about one division — are building roads in northern Laos, largely to improve the logistics on the approaches to Thailand. This penetration dates back to 1962. ...

Maoist activity in the Philippines has been endemic for 20-odd years and is still continuing.

In Indonesia Maoist guerrillas became active in 1965 and are now operating (with great difficulty) on Sumatra and Borneo, possibly on Celebes.

Early in 1971 Maoist guerrillas engaged in a people's war *en miniature* on Ceylon. This force has not yet been liquidated.

In the Middle East, Maoist-supported Arab guerrilla organizations tried repeatedly during 1970 to take power in Jordan and to provoke another Arab war with Israel. The Maoists, partly through Al Fatah, have been feeding a "liberation war" in Eritrea. They also have been active in southern Yemen and since 1970 have been infiltrating into Muscat and Oman.

In Africa the Chinese are building a railroad from the Tanzania coast to the copper mines in Zambia. They seem to be running guerrilla training camps, especially in Tanzania, and they assign instructors to all camps where the African governments allow them in. Brazzaville Congo and Guinea, and possibly Gambia and Zambia, are available as base areas. The Maoists carry on guerrilla operations in Mozambique, Angola, Cabinda, and Bissau-Guinea.

In Europe, the Maoists are at present very active in Paris and are working toward a new "Red May."

Most of these operations are as yet in their preparatory phases and some are merely diversionary. But clearly, aside from their objectives vis-a-vis the USSR, Japan and the U.S., Peking wishes to "Maoize" Southeast Asia, minus "Indochina" which they are willing to cede to Hanoi, and to dislocate India which conceivably would be divided along ethnic lines, with most or all ethnic groups under Maoist rule.

It has been said that Maoist strategy has not been very successful. This is highly debatable because the play has barely progressed beyond its prologue. The point is, however, that a weakening or termination of U.S. presence in Asia or only the abandonment of Viet Nam and of our Asian SEATO allies would enable the Maoists to branch out in all directions and to pluck the fruits which they have been planting during the last two decades.

If America leaves or gives its tacit blessing to the Maoists, several Asian governments will seek USSR protection (which will be freely given), and others will throw in their lot with Maoist China.

The "domino theory" may be viewed with skepticism. But the fact is that Maoist forces are already emplaced in

THE TIGER IN ASIA

We in America have those among us who are unable to "see the tiger" which is seeking to devour most of Asia.

The tiger, of course, is Red China.

The People's Republic of China intends to control the destiny of Asia, particularly Southeast Asia. Chinese historical precedents, population pressures, security interests, and ideological drives have made the region a prime target for Peking's expansionists policies.

Using both direct and indirect methods, China intends to establish a buffer area for the security of its own territory, to force withdrawal of Western power and influence. Ultimately the Chinese would set up "puppet" regimes which would follow the leadership and dictates of Peking.

By establishing its unchallenged supremacy in Southeast Asia, Peking would attain both ideological and strategic goals.

Communism would expand its hold on millions of Asians. China would be surrounded by weak allied states. It could create its "coprosperity sphere" — as Japan attempted in World War II — by which the growing industrial power of China would be nurtured by the raw materials and markets of Asian satellites.

Some Americans, including influential Senators and journalists, refuse to see this tiger.

Because Chinese Communist capabilities at present are limited, they discount Peking's intentions.

Congressman Zablocki of Wisconsin before House of Representatives, January 24, 1968.

73

most of the target countries. If the President's visit to Peking should result in sacrificing our allies or weakening the will of Peking's neighbors to resist Maoist aggression, then these forces will clearly expand in strength. Hence, the President must make it clear that we have no intention of abandoning our allies.

If we leave them now for some vaporous promises from Peking, we will find ourselves at some future date fighting under greater stress, at far greater costs and risks, and with much higher casualties, than if we stick to the strategy which, by and large, has contained Maoist aggression since 1949.

READING NUMBER 10

RED CHINA: MENACE OR MYTH?

(This reading originated as a discussion at The Center for the Study of Democratic Institutions, involving Edwin O. Reischauer, J. W. Fulbright, Mark O. Hatfield and Masumi Ezaki. The Center is described by its chairman as an educational organization whose "object is to understand and to promote understanding of the basic issues that underlie the formulation of public policy.")

Reflect on these questions before reading:

1. In the following discussion, what arguments are given to support the idea that China is not an aggressive nation?
2. Ambassador Reischauer claims that a factor he calls "culturalism" prevents China from extending its influence to other parts of the world. What is his point?
3. Do the participants explain why China's government believes American foreign policy is imperialistic and a threat to China's security?
4. What changes in American foreign policy are recommended?

*Elaine H. Burnell (ed.), *Asian Dilemma: United States, Japan and China* (Santa Barbara, California: Center for the Study of Democratic Institutions, 1969), pp. 81-89. Reprinted with permission from *Asian Dilemma,* a publication of the Center for the Study of Democratic Institutions in Santa Barbara, California.

Ambassador Reischauer: In the United States the chief emphasis has been on the menace of China. It is strange that we Americans, far across the Pacific and a much stronger nation, should fear China in a way that the Japanese do not. Frankly, I would side with the Japanese. I think they view China much more realistically than we.

EDWIN O. REISCHAUER was born in Tokyo in 1910 and educated at Oberlin College and Harvard University. He studied in France, Japan, and China on a Fellowship from the Harvard-Yenching Institute. He has served in the War Department, the United States Army, and the Department of State. Appointed Ambassador to Japan in 1961, he returned to Harvard in 1966. His books include *Japan Past and Present, The United States States and Japan, Wanted: An Asian Policy,* and *Beyond Vietnam.*

Senator Fulbright: We have based our policy and our feelings on certain assumptions. We assumed, of course, that all communist regimes were joined together indissolubly in a conspiratorial compact to conquer the world. And we have treated the communist countries as a monolithic entity of awesome power and frightening potential. It is not too surprising, then, that we have regarded China as a hostile and aggressive nation that is threatening to impose communism on Asia by force just as the Soviet Union imposed its ideology on central Europe.

Ambassador Reischauer: The real question we in America must face is not whether China as a communist power would like to see other people have revolutions. We must look at the record and decide if China is an expansionist, aggressive, militarily dangerous country. My own answer would be that she is not a great danger.

J. W. FULBRIGHT, senior Senator from Arkansas and Chairman of the Senate Foreign Relations Committee, was born in Sumner, Missouri, in 1905. He holds an A.B. from the University of Arkansas, an A.B. and an M.A. from Oxford University, and an LL.D. from George Washington University. He was elected to Congress in 1943 after serving as President of the University of Arkansas. Among his publications are  *Prospects for the West, Old Myths and New Realities,* and *The Arrogance of Power.*

Senator Fulbright: I do not see that the present Chinese government has made any serious attempt to expand its territory beyond its present borders. The Chinese forces that fought us in Korea are no longer there. North Korea has, in fact, become less pro-Chinese and more neutral in the Sino-Soviet dispute in recent years. Nor did Chinese forces remain in India. And in the case of Tibet, the Chinese took over a territory that both Peking and the Nationalist government have long regarded as Chinese.

Ambassador Reischauer: We do have to face the reality that the Chinese have gone across their borders on three occasions, but we should look at each case from their point of view, not just from our own. I think they honestly thought of their entry into the Korean War as self-defense, remembering that this was the route by which Japan had extended its empire into China. They thought we were coming to attack *them* in North Korea. Against the Indians their military action amounted to a small correction of the border, and I don't think they had any intention of seizing and trying to hold parts of India. Today they do have a certain number of labor troops, but not combatants, in Vietnam. Again they probably view their presence there more in terms of self-defense than of conquest. ...

Senator Hatfield: I would think that the greatest threat to China's neighbors is not the unlikely possibility of invasion by Chinese forces but the threat of internal subversion encouraged by Peking.

Quiet, Please!

Senator Fulbright: China has certainly encouraged and supported insurrections and wars of national liberation but, as far as I am aware, has not participated directly. There have been threats of direct participation, but China has not suited her actions to her words.

Certainly, the Peking government hopes that wars of national liberation will succeed not only in Vietnam but in Laos, Thailand, Burma, and other Asian countries. They have made no secret of their desire in this regard. But a

MARK O. HATFIELD, SR., was born in Dallas, Oregon, in 1922. Graduated from Willamette University, he holds a master's from Stanford University. He taught political science at Willamette and was Dean of Students there from 1950-1956. After a number of years in the State Senate, he became Governor of Oregon in 1959. A Republican, he was elected to the United States Senate in 1967 and is now senior Senator from Oregon. His book, *Not Quite So Simple,* was published in 1968.

desire to see such wars succeed, a desire that is no stronger than our desire to see them fail, is one thing. Ability to insure success is quite another.

Ambassador Reischauer: If we look at what the Chinese say about their present policies and what they do about them, I think we must be impressed that they talk about revolution throughout the world and not about conquest or aggression. They are happy to help other people have revolutions. They are glad to supply do-it-yourself kits to others. They don't talk much about going elsewhere and doing it for them, nor have they tried.

Senator Hatfield: Many experts have made the point that wars of national liberation can be successful only in a climate of political instability where the economic, social, and political grievances of the people are ignored or suppressed. Unless we send in enough men to constitute an occupation force, as we have in Vietnam, the American military cannot be expected to maintain stability in the face of these conditions. On the contrary, I believe it is demonstrable that our military presence heightens instability by stimulating the nationalistic sensitivities of the people.

American foreign policymakers could learn a lesson from the nursery rhyme: "All the king's horses and all the king's men couldn't put Humpty Dumpty together again." With all our military resources and all of our men, we cannot reconstruct a stability that has been shattered by political revolution. Like our Japanese colleagues, I think our most effective course would be to prevent the nations of Southeast Asia from falling into chaos by providing economic and technical assistance. If, in spite of our efforts, progress is too slow or political and social justice too remote, we must expect that communist-led revolutions may succeed.

Senator Fulbright: I suspect that the fears some Asians express about direct Chinese expansion or indirect Chinese intervention are often rationalizations, attempts to blame internal infirmities on external factors. Wars of national liberation can be and are supported from the outside. So are attempts to defeat them. But it seems to me that they are essentially home-grown products that sprout from complaints and frustrations, nourished by government in-effectiveness, lack of interest, and corruption.

I doubt that China presently could be successful as an expansionist military power even if she desired to be one. The Chinese have a powerful land army capable of defending the mainland against almost any combination of forces, but if mobile forces, strategically positioned, are necessary for expansion, it is we and not the Chinese who have that potential. If the evidence of a capacity and a desire to expand is the presence of a country's troops outside its own territory, what conclusion can we draw when the only Chinese soldiers outside China are engineer and air defense units in North Vietnam while, in Asia alone, we have more than half a million troops in South Vietnam, over fifty thousand in South Korea, and some forty thousand in Thailand? What about our naval and air installations in Japan, the Philippines, Taiwan, Okinawa, Guam, and elsewhere?

Ambassador Reischauer: The Chinese are a fundamentally inward-looking civilization, and well they might be. They are by all odds the largest unit of people in the world. One of the great miracles of human history is that this huge mass of people has held together as a single, successful political unit for the better part of two thousand years. Since they are part of such a large unit, the Chinese have always tended to look in at themselves rather than out at the fringe of barbarians beyond China. They have regarded all foreigners either as closer, semi-civilized barbarians like the other East Asians or as more distant, hopelessly barbaric peoples like those in Europe.

Today China has great problems that make her all the more inward-looking, and it seems improbable that she will turn outward for quite some time. China suffers from gigantism. Being a nation of seven to eight hundred million people has great disadvantages, and the problems connected with her huge size and her low economic base will keep China absorbed in herself for the foreseeable future.

The Chinese are also susceptible to a phenomenon I call culturalism. It's a little different from nationalism, closer perhaps to the popular modern term, racism. They are egocentric and have great difficulty extending their influence to other parts of the world. Their efforts in Africa illustrate this problem of culturalism. Africans very soon found out that the Chinese are every bit as arrogant as the whites. They are not interested in the black people as such and are unwilling as yet to accept them as equals. Culturalism will make even their more subtle efforts to help worldwide revolution somewhat unlikely to succeed.

When we consider all these realities, present as well as past, I think we have greatly overestimated the threat of China and have been wrong to base so much of our effort on the concept of containment.

CHINA ISOLATION IMPOSSIBLE

The Chinese are a great and vital people who should not remain isolated from the international community. In the long run, no stable and enduring international order is conceivable without the contribution of this nation of more than 700 million people.

President Richard M. Nixon on March 9, 1970.

Mr. Ezaki: Two years ago I visited Peking. I am a pro-American politician, and I was not sure the Chinese would welcome me. I went there to find out whether there was any possibility of war breaking out between the United States and China. Perhaps because I was a director of the Japanese National Self-Defense Agency, the Peking

81

government decided to show me the People's Liberation Army. I do not know, but they may have been trying to send a message to the United States through me. In any case, what I saw primarily were land forces equipped with obsolete arms. Their tanks, for example, were vintage 1958.

They gave me a demonstration of guerrilla warfare. There was a shack. One of the trainees opened the door and went in. There was an explosion. Then the trainee, acting hungry, opened a pot on the stove. Another explosion. He grabbed a cigarette. Another explosion. Obviously the Chinese were trying to tell me that they would resort to guerrilla warfare if their country should be invaded.

All the methods and equipment I saw were primitive in the extreme. Their army could never face the tremendous military power of the United States in conventional warfare.

What struck me, however, was that here were close to eight hundred million people being driven by their leaders in a single direction. Their resentment against both the Soviet Union and the United States was being fanned at every opportunity. All the Chinese women I saw were dressed in one color, brownish black. They wore no lipstick. Obviously they were thinking in terms of preparing for war.

In China isolation produces vast ignorance of the outside world. My guide was a student at Peking University, one of the two largest universities in China. This young intellectual told me: "You people are still under American occupation. We understand that you are still living in poverty and are starving." To have an intellectual attending one of the great universities say that to me was appalling. Complete isolation and ignorance are fearful things. And these are the people being contained and prevented from having outside contact by the United States.

Senator Hatfield: I believe Peking's belligerency and militancy are not just the products of China's century of humiliation. I think they are also frustrated reactions to our refusal to treat them as equals. One of the troubles with Americans is our propensity to think we are superior in every way. It's perfectly all right, for instance, for the United States to have "the bomb" because we are a peace-loving nation, but it's not all right for the Chinese to have it because they are barbarians with no concern for

MASUMI EZAKI, from Aichi Prefecture, was born in 1922 and graduated from Nippon University. He was elected to the House of Representatives in 1946 and has been re-elected eight times. He has served as Vice-Minister of Construction, Chairman of the Committee on Budget, and Director-General of the National Defense Agency and has occupied a number of positions within the Liberal Democratic Party. He is President of Imasen Electric Company and President of Ichinomiya Women's College.

human life. We think it's reasonable for the United States, under the Monroe Doctrine, to keep possibly hostile foreign nations away from our borders and out of our hemisphere. But when the Chinese rather impotently rant and rave and issue aggressive declarations about *our* military bases on *their* borders, we solemnly nod our heads and interpret their rhetoric as a determination to dominate Asia and, if possible, the world.

Just as we take a rather smug view of our moral superiority, we think that our institutions and political system must be inherently superior. Because they have worked remarkably well for us, we assume that they will inevitably be accepted by others. Certainly, some socialist systems have adapted capitalist principles and incentives to fit their own needs, but that doesn't mean all communist countries in the future will, or should.

Another thing we do is interpret Chinese rhetoric and actions in the worst possible light in order to confirm our own negative view of them. People tend to perform as others expect them to, and we risk creating self-fulfilling prophesies when we talk darkly of China's ''nuclear black-mail'' of her neighbors or sourly and loudly predict that she would be irresponsibly disruptive if she were admitted to the United Nations. No one expects American policy-

AS PEKING SEES THE U.S.
American imperialism's military encirclement of China

Source: *People's Daily*, Jan. 29, 1966

Symbols: 1. U.S. troops. 2. Naval bases. 3. Air bases. 4. Missile bases.
5. Aircraft carriers. 6. Nuclear submarines.

From Arthur Huck, *The Security of China*, The Institute for Strategic Studies, 1970.

makers to sit around thinking only good thoughts about the Chinese, but we do not need to give a perverse sanction to their hostile and belligerent actions by voicing nothing but dire expectations.

Senator Fulbright: Why shouldn't we discard the objective of containing China and, despite official disclaimers, isolating her as well? Or, to state it more accurately, why shouldn't we discard a policy of helping China to isolate herself in favor of seeing what can be done to involve China in Asia — and Asia in China — and to influence China to play a constructive and stabilizing, rather than a destructive and disruptive, role in the world?

The complex problems that revolve around the words

"Taiwan" and "Vietnam" will take years to unravel. In the meantime, it seems to me, everything possible should be done to clear the air — travel, trade, cultural relations. In addition, I think it would improve the atmosphere if the United States were to state clearly and unqualifiedly that this government is willing to recognize that the government of the People's Republic of China controls the mainland. ...

Senator Hatfield: Even if the United States abandons its isolation policy and substantially modifies its attempt at military containment, I have serious doubts that we will make much headway until we bring about a fundamental change in our attitude toward the Chinese. Until we learn to view the Chinese as people, abandon our self-righteous view that somehow we are above doing evil, and look at our conflicts as differences of opinion rather than as evidences of Chinese moral inferiority, the Chinese attitude toward us will probably remain belligerent and hostile.

Mr. Ezaki: After all, the United States is the world's greatest and wealthiest nation. Why can it not have the magnanimity to teach the Chinese that there is such a thing as *Pacem in Terris?* Nothing is as fearful as people living in ignorance. Why do we keep them out of the United Nations? Why can't we bring this vast mass of people into international society? They are communists today, sure, but they need not remain communists for all history. If we could only show them the value of freedom, if we could only show them the value of peace, then we would have a new China.

EXERCISE 5

CAUSE AND EFFECT RELATIONSHIPS

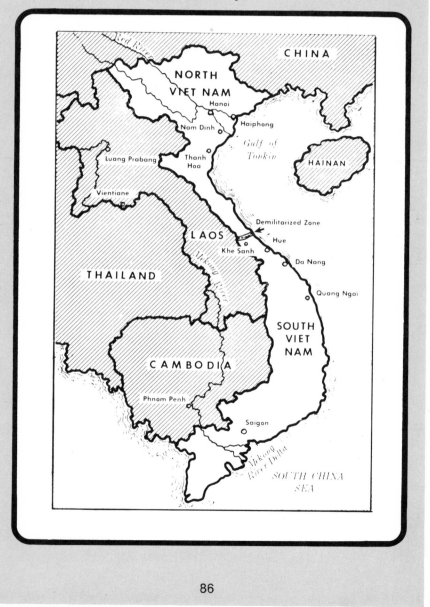

This discussion exercise provides practice in the skill of analyzing cause and effect relationships. Causes of human conflict and social problems are usually very complex. The following statements indicate possible causes for the Vietnam war. Rank them by assigning the number (1) to the most important cause, number (2) to the second most important, and so on until the ranking is finished. Omit any statements you feel are not causative factors. Add any causes you think have been left out. Then discuss and compare your decisions with other class members.

_____ a. Communist aggression against South Vietnam

_____ b. French Colonialism in Southeast Asia

_____ c. American aggression in South Vietnam

_____ d. Failure of the South Vietnamese government to extend land reform, education, medical care, and social justice to the peasant population.

_____ e. North Vietnamese aggression in South Vietnam

_____ f. Attempts by American and South Vietnamese leaders to solve Vietnam's social problems with military force.

_____ g. Corruption in South Vietnam's government

_____ h. Communist Chinese military intervention in South Vietnam

_____ i. American military intervention in South Vietnam

_____ j. Russian military intervention in South Vietnam

_____ k. Dictatorial or arbitrary government in South Vietnam

THE CONTAINMENT OF CHINA

by Walter H. Judd*

(Dr. Walter Judd is a teacher, lecturer and physician who spent several years as a medical missionary to China. He has served as a U. S. congressman from Minnesota and has received many religious and humanitarian awards for his work. Since 1963 he has served as a contributing editor to *The Reader's Digest.*)

These questions may help your understanding of the reading:

1. How does Dr. Judd describe U S. foreign policy toward China since 1950?
2. What does Dr. Judd think the current policy of the United States toward China should be?

*Dr. Walter H. Judd before the Senate Foreign Relations Committee on March 28, 1966.

Communist governments and their fronts are waging war against free peoples worldwide. At the moment the hot-test spot, and the test case for us, is Vietnam — as at other times the test case has been Japan, Greece, Berlin, Korea, Quemoy, Lebanon, Cuba.

But the issue is not Vietnam: it is how are disputes to be settled — by resolution through civilized means, or by armed force?

The state is not Vietnam; it is Asia — and ourselves and the world.

The problem is not Vietnam; it is aggressive Communist expansionism — this time from North Vietnam, backed up by the Soviet Union and Communist China.

Mr. Chairman, no great expansionist movement has ever stopped until it was checked. Our choice — with Red China just as it was with Japan and Hitler — is not between checking and not checking. The choice is whether to check early, while we can, and with allies — or try to check the aggression later when it is stronger, closer, and we have fewer and weaker friends and allies.

The urgent question, I think, is how to check it with least risk and cost.

U.S. CHINA POLICY SINCE 1950

Since the beginning of the Korean war in 1950, America's policy toward Communist China under the Truman, Eisenhower, Kennedy, and Johnson administrations has been a hard headed realistic attempt to protect the security interests of the United States by resisting any steps that would further increase Chinese Communist influence and power. An indispensable part of the policy has been to support and strengthen all non-Communist governments around China that are trying to preserve their independence and thereby to keep their manpower, territory, bases, and resources out of Communist control.

Some say that policy has failed because Red China is still there and is as hostile and as dedicated to world domination by armed force as ever. Yes, it is there; but where would the countries around Red China have been without this policy of containment of the aggressor and support of the free? There are great problems ahead for Korea, Taiwan, the Philippines, Burma, as well as South Vietnam, Malaysia, and Indonesia. But all of them are still free. And who can believe they would have been free, and with at least the possibility of solving their problems, if it had not been for our firm containment of China?

THE RUTHLESSNESS OF CHINA

If we, of the Republic of China, seem to have little faith in the often voiced hope of building bridges to the Communist mainland, it is because we have had long and bitter experience with Mao Tse-tung and his cohorts. We have learned, at a great cost, the worthlessness of his promises. We have experienced the fanatical ruthlessness with which he pursues his goals. We know that, even behind Chou En-lai's much publicized "smiles" lurks the unaltering intent to trap the free world, and especially the United States, into letting down its guard. We know, from their own boasts, that their aim is the subjugation of the world. With such an opponent, truces are meaningless.

James C. H. Chen, Ambassador of the Republic of China to the United States.

U.S. POLICY CHANGES

From what I have seen in the press, most of the changes in American policy toward Communist China proposed by various witnesses before this committee appear to be based on certain assumptions which do not seem to me to be justified:

1. That the Communist regime now in control of the China mainland is here to stay.

But the same was said of Hitler, of Khrushchev, of Sukarno, of Nkrumah. People are not so sure now that Castro will last forever. Despots generally appear invincible — "until the last 5 minutes."

2. That the United States is stubbornly keeping Red China isolated and therefore we are responsible for its hostility and belligerence. The reverse is the truth; it is Red China's hostility and belligerence in its international attitudes and actions, that are responsible for its isolation.

General George Marshall wrote on January 7, 1947,

after he had spent a year trying the very policies now being recommended of friendliness, conciliation, bringing the Chinese Communists into the Chinese Government and into the world community:

''I wish to state to the American people that in the deliberate misrepresentation and abuse of the action, policies, and purposes of our Government this propaganda (against the United States) has been without regard for the truth, without any regard whatsoever for the facts, and has given plain evidence of a determined purpose to mislead the Chinese people and the world and to arouse a bitter hatred of Americans.''

Mr. Chairman, if I may interject, it can perhaps be thought of in baseball terms. To the Communists, China is first base. The countries around China, where live a third of the people of the world, are second base. Africa and Latin America are third base. But ordinarily you don't go to third base to stop; you go to third base to try to get home. Homeplate, of course, is the United States and Western Europe. They proclaimed precisely this strategy as you know in the recent Lin Piao reaffirmation of the original statement made repeatedly by Mao Tse-tung.

Mr. Chairman, I come from Minnesota and Maury Wills is not one of our chief heroes up there. When he is on first base, do we say, ''Well, he is tough. Let's give him second base, and maybe that will please him so, and make him so grateful that he won't try to get to third base''?

No, we try to keep him on first base. In essence that is what our policy under four administrations has been — to keep Red China on first base. How do you accomplish that? We must not do anything to strengthen Red China. Secondly, we must do all we properly can to strengthen the countries around China that are resisting its expansion.

Mr. Chairman, I don't believe the American people will ever accept the assumption that any tyranny is here to stay, or that we will accept as permanent the subjugation of any people, no matter how powerful the despots may look at the moment.

The cause of Red China's hostility is not its isolation, but the Communist doctrine of the necessity for use of armed force to achieve world revolution. To remove China's isolation now would prove that the doctrine is correct and should be adhered to by them even more tenaciously.

3. That there is a better hope of getting Red China to change its attitudes and activities by giving in to it on matters like diplomatic recognition, trade, and admission to the United Nations than by resolute continuance of the policy of containment as long as Red China refuses to act like a responsible member of civilized society.

4. That changing our policy vis-a-vis Red China just might start an evolutionary process there.

But, of course, it might just as easily reduce the chances of such an evolutionary process. Everybody desires and hopes for "evolution" in Red China. The debate should be over what measures are most likely to produce it.

For example (a) giving Red China greater prestige, influence, entree; that is, making it stronger? Or keeping it as weak and isolated as possible?

(b) Concessions from its intended victims — like the United States? Or pressures from its present victims — the Chinese within Red China, those on Taiwan and in southeast Asia, Muslims in Indonesia and Malaysia, et cetera?

(c) Proving that Red China's truculence and stubborn defiance of the world succeeds? Or showing that it will fail?

(d) Taking the mountain — United Nations — to Mao? Or patiently and nonbelligerently insisting that Mao come to the mountain of better international conduct if he wants the benefits to Red China of membership in the international community?

What has caused the reported mellowing and evolution inside Yugoslavia, Rumania, the Soviet Union? Influences from without? Or their failures within?

If economic and other pressures from within and without are compelling some Communist governments to moderate their policies, at least toward their own people, shouldn't we keep the pressures up rather than reduce them by helping those Governments to solve their problems?

92

FIVE STEPS TOWARD A NEW U.S. - CHINA POLICY

by George McGovern*

(George McGovern has served as a U.S. Senator from South Dakota since 1963. He sought the Democratic presidential nomination for the 1968 election and after winning the nomination in 1972 was defeated by President Nixon in the November election. He is a severe critic of U.S. policies in Indochina. He was a decorated combat pilot during the second world war and taught history and political science at Dakota Wesleyan University before entering politics.)

Consider the following questions while reading:

1. Why does Senator McGovern think we should reassess our foreign policy toward China?
2. How does he suggest we solve the problem of U.S. recognition of the Taiwan government?
3. What five steps does the author recommend for a new U.S.-China policy?

*This reading is taken from an address delivered by Senator McGovern at the University of the Pacific in Stockton, California on January 24, 1971, and is reprinted with the author's permission.

It is time we began to assess China in realistic terms.

We must do so, first, because our actions and preparations for dealing with the China of our imaginations have damaged us far more than the China that is real either can or would.

We must do so because our policy, instead of responding to existing threats, tends to create threats which would otherwise not be posed.

And we must do so because we approach a new era, in which the consequences of continued efforts to isolate, encircle, and vilify China can be even more deadly than the costs of the past.

Let me suggest, then, several fundamental elements of a new posture toward China.

NO NEED FOR ABM

First, we should forego any plan to construct an area defense anti-ballistic missile system designed to nullify the budding Chinese deterrent force.

We have good enough reason to give up such plans on purely technical grounds. ...

But the implications for U.S.-China relations raise overwhelming support for the same conclusion. We do not need an anti-Chinese ABM, and its construction will harm immeasurably the prospects for nuclear stability.

China's attitude toward nuclear weapons has been brash in rhetoric but cautious in practice. Like other nuclear powers, they contend that their nuclear capability is developed solely to deter a nuclear attack from other countries.

Their nuclear tests have been accompanied by advocacy of nuclear disarmament and the creation of "nuclear-weapon-free" zones. They have made a unilateral commitment against their own first use of nuclear weapons — something the United States has never done. They upbraided the Soviet Union for "adventurism" following the Cuban missile crisis in 1962.

But if we still fear China's attitudes, there is no prospect at all that the Chinese will attain a nuclear force big enough or advanced enough to threaten our deterrent.

94

OUR CHINA POLICY HAS BEEN A FAILURE

Under any reasoned assessment our China policy has been a spectacular, costly failure.

Its architects and advocates have presented us with:

Two land wars in countries bordering China;

A military buildup which has reached nearly a million men on the eastern and southern borders of China;

The continued occupation by American ground or air forces of every country on those eastern and southern borders of China from Japan through Korea, Taiwan, Okinawa, the Philippines, South Vietnam, Cambodia, Laos, and Thailand;

Over 100,000 American dead in East Asia, and more than five times that many Americans wounded;

The physical devastation of broad areas of Korea, Vietnam, Laos, and Cambodia;

Direct responsibility for several million dead and wounded Asian women, children, old men, and other noncombatants who have found themselves on our anti-China battlefield;

The alienation of large segments of our own society who see the war in Indochina as an illegal, immoral venture; and

The distortion and disruption of our national economy, with an accompanying neglect of urgent domestic priorities.

Yet the People's Republic of China survives, grows stronger, and is recognized as reality by a steadily increasing proportion of the world community.

The illogic, the costs, and the failure of our policy should be enough to convince us that it ought to be changed.

Senator George McGovern before the Senate on March 24, 1971.

They need never doubt that any attack on the United States will bring immediate destruction to their own society, to all of their cities, to all of their painfully built industrial base, and to millions of their people.

Under such circumstances construction of an anti-Chinese ABM requires us to believe that Peking is ruled by fools and suicidal maniacs.

We cannot welcome any proliferation in these dangerous weapons. But neither can we stop the emergence of China as a nuclear force. We gain nothing and lose much, therefore, by attempting to deny China the ability to deter nuclear attack, by attempting to deny her the same protection we consider prudent and responsible for ourselves.

Second, our position on trade with China should be put on the same basis as U.S. trade with the Soviet Union and other communist nations in Eastern Europe. We must end the almost total embargo on trade which we have imposed for twenty years.

It is a relic of a futile and foolish attempt to bring down the communist government by isolating her from normal social and economic relations not only with the United States but with all free countries. Its primary victim has been the United States. It is costing us a vast market for our produce that is now being pre-empted by the Japanese and others while we keep our head stuck in the sand.

EXCHANGES BY SCIENTISTS

Third, as an effort to initiate travel and cultural contacts, an invitation should be made at the Warsaw talks, and eventually in open dialogue with the Peking government, for visitations to the United States by Chinese scientists, government officials, newspapermen, and similar groups.

We should begin, as well, to encourage American-Chinese natural scientists working in purely theoretical fields to resume their private contacts in China and to seek visas to visit their families, relatives, and friends from whom they have been separated for more than 20 years.

Fourth, we must address without equivocation the perplexing question of Chinese representation in the United Nations.

96

In a series of votes in the General Assembly during the last week of October, 1971, Communist China was seated in the United Nations and the Republic of China from Taiwan was expelled. The United States voted against the admission of Communist China and against the expulsion of the Republic of China.

"By golly, I do believe I see something there after all"

Prior to the next General Assembly meeting, the United States should enlist majority support for a resolution to recognize the People's Republic of China as the Legitimate occupant of China's seat in the United Nations General Assembly and on the Security Council.

On the question of Taiwan, we may consider a subsequent arrangement continuing membership in the U.N., but not of the Security Council, pending settlement on the island's status. We should abandon our effort to designate Chinese representation an "important question" requiring two-thirds approval.

Fifth, we should adopt a similar approach to the problem of recognition. Again, I can foresee no simple solution to the Taiwan issue. We should, however, be clear on one point: that our recognition of reality with respect to the Chinese civil war will, of itself, raise serious questions about Chiang Kai-shek's claim that he leads the government of any country.

He agrees with Peking's claim that Taiwan is part of China. If that issue is resolved positively then we must recognize that Taiwan, too, will live under the same government as the Mainland. If not, and there are some historical and ethnic reasons for such a view, then Chiang's claim to authority on the island will still derive only from the fact that he fled there and took and held power with brutal force after his defeat on the Mainland.

TAIWAN ISSUE NOT OURS TO DECIDE

In any case, the status of Taiwan is not ours to decide. We may hope for its resolution through international auspices or among the Chinese and Taiwanese people themselves. But we should move now to recognize the government in Peking and to seek diplomatic relations. Chinese acceptance of the Canada formula, in which Canada was obliged only to take note of the Chinese claim to Taiwan, sets a useful pattern which we could wisely pursue. The desperate need for growing knowledge, contact, and understanding should be denied no longer. ...

The heaviest responsibility facing the next president is to initiate and then press forward as rapidly as circumstances will allow, a dialogue with China of the sort that has made our relations with the Soviet Union, if not friendly, at least less dangerous to ourselves and to the world.

The search will require patience, skill, and understanding, as it has in the case of the Soviet Union. We have had, and will continue to have, profound differences of interest and outlook with both regimes. At the beginning we can expect that many of our initiatives will be met with scorn.

But we do have common interests. We share, I believe, a common aspiration for avoiding the confrontation which could end human life on this planet, for in that kind of conflict there can be no winners.

And we can share a respect for national boundaries in all parts of the world, and a hope that what competition there is between conflicting ideologies beyond those boundaries will be conducted in peace. We can achieve that if we can on both sides replace hysteria with reason and temper our passion with common sense.

A nation as rich and powerful as the United States can readily afford to move in a spirit of understanding and respect.

If we are truly committed to truth, and if we are *determined* to shed the burdens of past mistakes, then we can clearly do no less.

RECOGNIZING ETHNOCENTRIC STATEMENTS

This discussion exercise is designed to promote one's ability to identify ethnocentric statements. *Ethnocentrism* is the tendency for people to feel their group, culture, or nation is superior and to judge others by one's own *frame of reference.* Frame of reference means the standards and values a person accepts because of his life experience and the culture he grows up in. A Moslem in Pakistan, for example, is likely to view many things differently than a Christian in England.

Ethnocentrism has promoted much misunderstanding and conflict. It helps emphasize cultural differences and the notion that your nation's institutions are superior. Education, however, should stress the similarities of the human condition throughout the world and the basic equality and dignity of all men.

In order to avoid future wars and violence, people must realize how *ethnocentrism* and *frame of reference* limit ability to be objective and understanding. Consider each of the following statements carefully. Mark (E) for any statement you feel is ethnocentric. Mark (N) for any statement you believe is not ethnocentric. Then discuss and compare your judgments with those of other class members.

(E) = Ethnocentric
(N) = Not Ethnocentric

_____ 1. Can America trust the Communists to keep an agreement? Of course not. And we may be sure they do not trust us.

_____ 2. The Greek government is an antidemocratic force unfit for membership in the Atlantic Alliance.

_____ 3. The U. S. leads the world in doing the impossible. History reflects no other national progress of such dimension. America must preserve a heritage that proved the soundness of Western culture.

_____ 4. Since Fidel Castro established communism in Cuba, he has spared no effort to expand communism to the rest of Latin America.

_____ 5. The people of Vietnam are not yet fully capable of governing themselves without some assistance from the U. S.

_____ 6. The belligerent anti-American statements made by Red China's spokesmen during the past year leave no doubt that the U. S. is Communist China's No. 1 enemy.

_____ 7. If America continues to spend more money every year on military defense than on programs to solve our social problems, we will suffer spiritual death.

_____ 8. If the world can act toward China with understanding and generosity, it will be on the way to a solution of the great problems of Asia.

_____ 9. God has been preparing the Christian world for a thousand years to bring spiritual and social justice to all the world.

Selected Periodical Bibliography

For statements on American foreign policy, the interested student should examine recent issues of **The Department of State Bulletin, Current History** and **Foreign Affairs.** These publications have not been added to the following bibliography.

Charles Benson — "A Strategic Alternative," *National Review,* November 17, 1970, pp. 1206-10.

Bernard J. Burnham — "What Liberals Don't Understand About Vietnam," *National Review,* January 26, 1971, pp. 77-80.

Frank Church — "Vietnam: Disengagement Now," *Vital Speeches,* November 1, 1969, pp. 34-39.

John Sherman Cooper — "The Need For NATO," *Vital Speeches,* January 15, 1969, pp. 194-96.

Angier Biddle Duke — "Military Policy and Foreign Policy, a Time to Review," *Vital Speeches,* August 1, 1969, pp. 628-31.

J. W. Fulbright — "The Most Powerful Country — The Most Populous Country," *Vital Speeches,* February 15, 1969, pp. 258-62.

Leslie H. Gelb — "Today's Lessons from the Pentagon Papers," *Life,* September 17, 1971, pp. 34-36.

Alan H. Grossman — "China and the U.S.: The Twain Shall Meet," *Harpers,* October, 1971, pp. 86-94.

Averell Harriman — "Hopeful Talks With the Soviet Leaders," *Life,* February 5, 1971, pp. 30-31.

Mark O. Hatfield — "United States—China Relations: A Greater Understanding," *Vital Speeches,* March 15, 1969, pp. 322-26.

Stanley Hoffman — "Vietnam and Western Europe," *New Republic,* January 30, 1971, pp. 18-23.

George Hunt — "Our Four Star Military Mess," *Life,* June 18, 1971, pp. 50-68.

Henry M. Jackson — "Russia Has Not Changed Her Ways," *Reader's Digest,* June, 1969, pp. 91-95.

Herman Kahn — "Why U.S. Must Stay in Asia," *U.S. News and World Report,* February 8, 1971, pp. 60-64.

Melvin Laird	"Are We to Become a Second Rate Power?" *Vital Speeches,* May 15, 1970, pp. 452-56.
	"U.S. Strategy Beyond Vietnam," *U.S. News and World Report,* May 17, 1971, pp. 27-35.
Life	"Inside China," April 30, 1971. (special issue)
Look	"American Militarism: Who Profits? Who Pays? Who Commands? Who Dies?" August 12, 1969, pp. 13-56.
	"American Militarism: The Defense Establishment," August 26, 1969, pp. 17-44.
Eugene McCarthy	"A Kind Word for the Military," *Life,* March 5, 1971, p. 38.
	"Pentagon Papers," *New Republic,* July 10, 1971, pp. 14-17.
Malcolm Mackintosh	"Clues to Soviet Policy," *U.S. News and World Report,* February 2, 1970, pp. 66-69.
Hans J. Morgenthau	"Nixon's Foreign Policy," *New Republic,* March 21, 1970, pp. 23-25.
Bill Moyers	"Vietnam: What is Left of Conscience?" *Saturday Review,* February 23, 1971, pp. 20-21.
Charles J. V. Murphy	"What is Behind Red China's Smile?" *Reader's Digest,* October, 1971, pp. 69-73.
New Republic	"One China," April 24, 1971, pp. 5-6.
Bernard Nossiter	"Does Foreign Aid Really Aid?" *Harpers* February, 1970, pp. 61-63.
John R. Rarick	"Rhodesia: U.S. Foreign Policy?" *Vital Speeches,* May 1, 1970, pp. 434-37.
Stanley R. Resor	"United States Forces in Europe," *Vital Speeches,* May 15, 1970, pp. 456-59.
William P. Rodgers	"Foreign Policy and the United Nations," *Vital Speeches,* November 1, 1971, pp. 34-38.
	"Foreign Relations: Disarmament," *Vital Speeches,* May 1, 1969, pp. 420-25.
	"U. S. Policy in the Middle East," *Vital Speeches,* January 1, 1970, pp. 165-67.
Saturday Review	"Toward a Military Welfare State?" March 27, 1971, pp. 26-27.
Arthur Schlesinger, Jr.	"The Necessary Amorality of Foreign Affairs," *Harpers,* August, 1971, pp. 72-77.

Edgar Snow

"Talks With Chou En-lai," *New Republic,* March 27, 1971, pp. 20-23.

Adm. Elmo R. Zumwalt, Jr.

"Where Russian Threat Keeps Growing," *U.S. News and World Report,* September 3, 1971, pp. 72-77.

Acknowledgments

illustration and picture credits

Page

2   Reprinted with permission from Arthur Schlesinger, Jr.

5   Reprinted by permission from **The Christian Science Monitor** (c) 1969 The Christian Science Publishing Society. All Rights Reserved.

7   Justus in the **Minneapolis Star.** Reprinted with permission from the **Minneapolis Star.**

11   Burck in the **Chicago Sun-Times.** Reprinted with permission from the **Chicago Sun-Times.**

15   Justus in the **Minneapolis Star.** Reprinted with permission from the **Minneapolis Star.**

30   Herblock in **The Washington Post.** Reprinted with permission from Herblock Cartoons.

32   (c) 1969 by The New York Times Company. Reprinted by permission.

46   Reprinted by permission of **New York Post** (c) 1971, New York Post Corporation.

52   Reprinted with permission from the office of Senator Strom Thurmond.

54   Reprinted from **National Review** with permission, 150 East 35 Street, New York, N.Y. 10016.

64   Corky in the **Los Angeles Times.** Copyright, 1971, Los Angeles Times. Reprinted with permission.

71   Curtis in the **Milwaukee Sentinel.** Reprinted with permission.

75   Reprinted with permission from The Center for the Study of Democratic Institutions.

78   Justus in the **Minneapolis Star.** Reprinted with permission from the **Minneapolis Star.**

79   Reprinted with permission from The Center for the Study of Democratic Institutions.

84   Reprinted with permission from The Center for the Study of Democratic Institutions.

86   From **The Security of China** by Arthur Huck published in UK by Chatto & Windus and in United States by Columbia University Press, for The International Institute for Strategic Studies.

88   Reprinted with permission from **Congressional Quarterly.**

93   Reprinted with permission from the office of Senator George McGovern.

98   Sanders in **The Milwaukee Journal.** Reprinted with permission from **The Milwaukee Journal.**

meet
the editors

GARY E. McCUEN, currently a social studies teacher at Eisenhower Senior High School in Hopkins, Minnesota, received his A.B. in history from Ripon College, and has an M.S.T. degree in history which he received from Wisconsin State University in Eau Claire, Wisconsin.

DAVID L. BENDER is a history graduate from the University of Minnesota. He also has an M.A. in government from St. Mary's University in San Antonio, Texas. He has taught social problems at the high school level and is currently working on additional volumes for the Opposing Viewpoints Series.